MW00736399

Steven Ehrlich

architects

Steven Ehrlich architects

introduction by
Joseph Giovannini

essay by
Steven Ehrlich

RIZZOLI
NEW YORK

First published in the United States of America in 1998 by
Rizzoli International Publications, Inc.
300 Park Avenue South, New York, NY 10010

Copyright © 1998 Rizzoli International Publications, Inc.

All rights reserved.
No part of this publication may be reproduced in any
manner whatsoever without permission in writing from
Rizzoli International Publications, Inc.

Ehrlich, Steven, 1946–
        Steven Ehrlich Architects / introduction by Joseph Giovannini;
        essay by Steven Ehrlich.
        p.   cm.
        Includes bibliographical references
        ISBN 0-8478-2075-0
        1. Ehrlich, Steven, 1946–   .   2. Steven Ehrlich Architects.
        3. Architecture, Modern—20th century—California, Southern.
        4. Vernacular architecture—Influence.   I. Title.
        NA737.S642e47   1998
        720'.92—dc21   98-11898
                                                                      CIP

Design by Tracey Shiffman, Los Angeles
Front jacket illustration: Robertson Branch Library (Tom Bonner)
Frontispiece illustration: Ahmadu Bello University Theater (Steven Ehrlich)
Back jacket illustration: Addition to Neutra Beach House (Julius Shulman/
        David Glomb)
Illustration this page: Robertson Branch Library (Tom Bonner)

Printed in Singapore

contents

Djene Mosque, rooftop

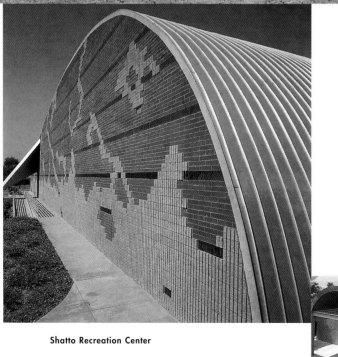

Shatto Recreation Center

Addition to Neutra Beach House

A Tense, Teasing, and Contradictory Balance

Joseph Giovannini

The career issues Steven Ehrlich has faced for nearly twenty years in Southern California are those that confront all architects of good faith and strong ambition—the anxiety of influence, the dilemma of synthesis, the search for identity, and the emergence of voice. One difference between Ehrlich and many other architects, however, has been the embarrassment of riches—the sheer number and quality of influences, some of which seem contradictory and difficult to reconcile. He came to California with an unusual education and work background; California had multiple identities of its own.

A member of the draft-chased Vietnam War generation, Ehrlich joined the Peace Corps in 1969 and embarked on what would prove a six-year sojourn in Africa. In Marrakech, he worked for several years in the city's department of urbanism and architecture before traveling through other Saharan and sub-Saharan countries. In Nigeria he taught architecture at the Ahmadu Bello University; and, inspired by the country's mud-walled compounds, built a five hundred–seat, in-the-round courtyard theater surrounded by cylindrical, mud-packed, thatch-roofed buildings decorated with hand-sculpted reliefs. During the six years, he became an observer of vernacular architecture—often the buildings that caught the lens of his camera were built of mud dug from their sites—and he came to admire the directness, simplicty, and ecological wisdom of earth-based construction. Ehrlich acquired an abiding respect for the courtyard and the urban square as the organizational principle for the house and city: he observed it was a pooling device that brought people together and helped them socialize, fusing their sense of community.

California was also territory with a strong architectural history—a domain where many significant architects had already left their mark. The inspired tradition of modernism in California dates from Irving Gill and includes Frank Lloyd Wright, Lloyd Wright and three, going on four, subsequent generations—Harwell Harris,

Gregory Ain, A. Quincy Jones, Ray Kappe, and many others. R. M. Schindler's and Richard Neutra's buildings especially have haunted drafting rooms in Southern California: their buildings represent an architecture that rests lightly on the land. Schindler, so concerned about the three-dimensionality of space, pursued designs that were as aerial as they were rooted, and Neutra dematerialized walls to erase boundaries between inside and out.

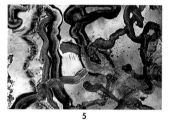

5

But any architect practicing in Los Angeles currently faces the example of Frank Gehry, who in fact diverges from the modernist mainstream in significant respects: the aesthetic is based on precedents from art rather than architecture culture, an approach Gehry cultivated through his association first with artists based in and around Venice, California, and later with those on the East Coast. Ehrlich originally established his own practice in the rough, gritty beachside community of Venice, and fell in with a similar crowd of artists. Their sensibility influenced his, as it did Gehry's. He collaborated with them on numerous projects in ways that significantly altered the design.

6

One spirit of Southern California, abstract expressionist Sam Francis, said that it is the individual who always carries the idea, and Ehrlich has been a living intersection of academic modernism, African vernacular, California modernism, Frank Gehry, Venice's light and space artists, and the larger contemporary architecture discourse. So before Ehrlich even approaches the yellow sheet of trace at the drafting table, many influences are ebbing and flowing through his mind and hand, and they alternately recede and advance in his projects. How he assimilates these influences and then forges them into an individual vision is the salient question for understanding his design.

The Kalfus studio (1980–81) is the most classically modernist design in his opus. The point of departure for the house was not only the hillside site in Hollywood and its long view over Los Angeles, but the main house on the

7

property—a flat-roofed, reductivist house by Richard Neutra with floor-to-ceiling, end-to-end vanishing glass walls. This was an example of what might today be called transparent minimalism. Ehrlich responded with a simple cubic volume at the far end of the property, composed with an exterior staircase asymmetrically placed on the garden facade. Sunlight, projected through its grated metal steps, casts geometrically laced shadows on the plain stucco surface. The two-story interior volume faces a soaring gridded wall of glass, with a northern exposure suitable for an artist's studio. The structure, which has a surprisingly small footprint, is remarkable for its disciplined simplicity and purity, and for its crisp abstraction. It was conceived at a time when architects in the United States were slipping into the lavender palette and classicist vocabulary of postmodernism. In that context, the effort was fresh and individualistic: Ehrlich was marching to his own drum rather than to the beat of the national press based in the East.

The abstract planes forming clean cubic volumes would remain a recurrent element in his vocabulary, though Ehrlich submits the idea to a progressive transformation. In the three-story Hollywood Hills Miller-Nazarey house (1984–86),

8

he erodes one corner of the prism on the ground floor next to the pool and garden, so that it can be closed by either a set of sliding glass doors, or shoji screens, or left completely open to the domestic Eden. In his own Santa Monica house (1987–88) and the Gold-Friedman house (1989–91) down the street, he breaks up the three-story masses into highly plastic compositions of asymmetrically cubic volumes that recede and advance as the houses step up the hillside slope. (At the rear, the entire volumes of the houses complement the sloping hillside, forming enclosed outdoor spaces reminiscent of the courtyards he experienced in North Africa.) Fragmenting the cubic mass into parts gives Ehrlich a formal vocabulary with which he can easily respond to interior programmatic needs and to the demands of the site. Sections and elevations resemble Schindler's abstract hill-

9

side projects from the 1930s.

The idea of shifted cubic masses is much transformed in Ehrlich's Schulman house (1989–92), but not because of greater plasticity. Within the asymmetrically poised volumes, Ehrlich nests glass walls composed of horizontal mullions that meet at mitered corners—similar to the disappearing corners of Frank Lloyd Wright's Freeman house and Schindler's houses of the 1920s. At the entrance, he also uses poured-in-place concrete that recalls Schindler's early use of concrete in courses that express horizontal pours. The important advance in the Schulman house is the hybridization of three materials and building vocabularies; the composite of concrete, stucco, and wood represents a juxtaposition of machine-tooled abstraction and craft traditions. The wood-framed sliding glass doors and the stone terraces outside the dining room and study recall traditional Japanese architecture: "Japan is always in my consciousness," says Ehrlich, who had, before beginning the design, made four trips to Japan for the Futiko-Tamagowon project in Tokyo. By extending two wings of the house so that they embrace the sycamore and waterspill and rectangular pool in the front yard, he creates a landscaped entrance forecourt. The barrier between indoors and outdoors dissolves as the rooms orient to the outside, as though in a state of architectural meditation.

Ehrlich's vocabulary of cubic volumes evolves dramatically in the Benenson house (1996–98) in Rustic Canyon, where the entire volume of the stepped two-story house is broken by elongated cubes of various heights that push and pull the plan parallel to the direction of the cubes' slide. Some of the cubic forms interrupting the building's mass are thin enough to seem like Mondrianesque lines cast in syncopated boogie-woogie rhythms: Ehrlich liberates the house into a play of form by bringing the asymmetrical disposition of cubic volumes into the de Stijl–like composition. The cubes are not simply visually strong: they become agents breaking up the mass of the house; volumes start slipping with planes to the outside, pushing parts into and

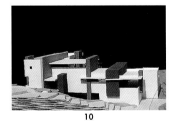

10

out of the yard, like forces. The abstractly handsome but static form of the Kalfus studio has transformed from a box into dynamic abstract shapes that impart movement to the plan, encouraging the house to engage in a more active relationship to the yard.

The richness of the Kalfus studio relied on simplicity to bring out the play of light and shadow on its surfaces, but, building by building, Ehrlich moves in the direction of complexity—first with the plastic complexity of his own house and the Gold-Friedman house, and then with the mixed language of the Schulman house. The Benenson house dynamizes the language.

Although Ehrlich has explored the potential of cubic volumes in numerous projects, they do not constitute a pat formal vocabulary that he applies to each commission. If the Kalfus studio of the early 1980s represents one design paradigm, Ehrlich finds another some five years later, as represented by the Shatto Recreation Center (1987–90). The premise of its design was a radical departure.

11

Ehrlich recalls that one of his teachers at Rensselaer Polytechnic Institute, sculptor George Rickey, said that a curved line is especially exciting as it accelerates or decelerates. Like the Kalfus studio, the Shatto Recreation Center is one big room with a number of ancillary spaces, but while the basic volume at Kalfus is static, the space in Shatto is dynamic: Ehrlich created an arched roof without a single radius point, which establishes the ever-changing profile of a rolling wave: he likes to say he brought a feeling of softness to an urban place. Ehrlich invited Venice painter Ed Moses to collaborate on developing a patterned wall by mixing and manipulating a palette of fluted sandstone, red brick, and shiny black-glazed blocks into a textured surface, so that the interior and exterior walls, too, change on all sides. Moses broke out of the normal grid lines, creating patterns that seem to crawl across the surfaces like snails. Ehrlich opened the design by integrating an artist's energy, insight, and insolence, invigorating what is all too often a closed and stiff architectural process with the artist's gestural spontaneity.

12

13

After Shatto, geometries that change internally or in relationship to others enter Ehrlich's conceptual framework. In the Child Care Center (1992–95), the architect fronts and backs his 9,000-square-foot building with long curved walls whose convex sides face one another. The heights of opposite points on the paired walls vary: the highest point on the front corresponds to the lowest on the back, and vice versa. Roof glu-lam beams spanning the two opposing glass and masonry walls then form an undulating surface. Between the convex walls and waving roof forms, the space constantly changes. Ehrlich underscores the metamorphosing geometric character of the space decoratively: a long colonnade of pipe columns on the play yard side of the building is painted in the chromatic gradient of the rainbow, and colored-glass windows waft over the back windows like clouds of free-form color.

In his design for the Paul Cummins Library (1995–96) at Crossroads, a private school in Santa Monica, Ehrlich and his partner, Nick Seierup, used changing geometries to take the form of diagonals rather than curves. The basic parti of the small library is simple, with offices and classrooms on the first floor, and a reading loft and stacks on the second. What distinguishes the building are the small but strategic liberties they take with the steel frame, tilting the rear wall at one angle, and the side wall at another: the roof, at a right angle to both, consequently tilts and slopes. The entire space of the building, inside and out, then, is energized by leaning walls set off against an otherwise orthogonal geometry. The whole structure is conventionally built, but the slight shifts quietly radicalize form and space, sending them into dynamic equilibrium. A glass cube at the front of the library on the ground floor serves as a periodical lounge, which acts as a socializing catalyst within a parking lot that is an all-purpose chatter yard. In this existing parking courtyard, Ehrlich and Seierup create a solid rather than a void.

At the Robertson Branch Library (1993–97), Ehrlich creates another con-

14

15

16

stantly changing shape, the hull of a boat that opens toward the top like a V. The vessel, then, flares as it rises, and comes to a point at both ends. Ehrlich drops this two-and-a-half-story shape through the two-story-structure, so that it forms a sky-lit stairwell from the first to the second floor. Again the parti is simple, with offices and a meeting room on the ground floor, and the reading loft and stacks on the second. In addition to choosing a geometry that changes in all three dimensions, Ehrlich mixes geometries by using the ship-shaped cone as an interruption in an otherwise placid box. The Vesuvian gesture, clad in patinated copper, erupts within the elevated box, becoming the kind of street-side road sign typical of strip architecture in Los Angeles and other car-oriented cities. The building at once acknowledges the deconstructivist strategy of crossing two noncoincident geometries simultaneously within the same building, and cultivates the commercial vernacular within a building type normally considered institutional and cultural: Ehrlich is mixing messages as well as geometries.

By creating a state of spatial flux with the noncoincident geometries, Ehrlich unlocks the usual registration of a building's coordinates, creating an indeterminate architectural condition. He achieves a comparable indeterminacy in the several projects where he has taken a found space and fitted it for a new program. In a Greyhound bus terminal in Santa Monica, transformed into a gym called the BUS

17

Wellness Center (1995–96), Ehrlich and Seierup weave the new exercise rooms, juice bar, changing rooms, lockers, and plumbing into the old structure, and exhibit rather than hide all the seams. For the revised plumbing services, they cut through the existing terrazzo floors and poured black concrete along the path. An episodic collage of mixed materials emerges, telling a tale of transformation: the original dilated space and brick walls of a bare-bones 1950s-vintage bus station acquires a denser character as Ehrlich and Seierup expose existing tapered steel girders and build interior garage doors into walls surfaced in

18

particle board and galvanized steel. Artist Philip Vourvoulis contributes to the environmental collage with a cast-glass countertop in the juice bar area perched like a precarious slab of thin ice. Ehrlich layers new on old to achieve a shifting, asymmetrical composition.

Whenever the program allows, Ehrlich creates a socializing space similar to the courtyards and squares he encountered in North Africa. In the bus depot turned gym, exercise spaces and lockers open to an informal interior atrium furnished with a canteen. The periodical lounge of the Paul Cummins Library serves a comparable function, like a fishtank of people in a parking lot swimming with cars. In the hillside projects, he cultivates the bowl of space between the uphill slope and the house as an outside common.

But the development of the courtyard or plaza is at its most explicit in larger projects, such as the 100,000-square-foot Sony Music Entertainment West Coast Headquarters in Santa Monica (1991–92), where the three separate low-rise office buildings, each a different shape, all orient to a landscaped plaza where a café catalyzes the social life. These outdoor courts are especially appropriate in Southern California as spaces that collect people on their way to and from desk and parking. Acknowledging that the streets are speedy thoroughfares for cars rather than pedestrians, he makes strong rhetorical gestures that can be glimpsed at forty miles per hour on the street, and introverts the site to cultivate focused community space. In DreamWorks SKG Animation Studios (1996–98), a 320,000-square-foot campus (with a planned second phase bringing the total square footage to nearly 500,000) for the famous animation company in Glendale, each of the five buildings is organized around a court, with all elevator cores opening to the courts. All courts spill into a common plaza. The way-finding is done through the hierarchy of outdoor spaces. Given the anomie of the car-oriented streets of Los Angeles, Ehrlich uses the courtyards as a way of creating and intensifying a sense of

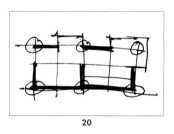

20

community. The urbanism is introverted within the project rather than open to the surrounding streets.

Perhaps it is not surprising that the design voice that is emerging from the matrix of influences coursing in Ehrlich's ecosystem is tending to multiplicity—that is, different forms, materials, geometries, and even idioms coexist in juxtapositions that celebrate their difference. Ehrlich is not trying to merge the differences into single, blended images, but suspends them in a state of architectural individuality. In the Robertson Library, for example, he embeds the hull-shaped cone within a plain elevated box, and each retains its identity (though each is changed, and charged, by the presence of the other). The two paradigms represented by the Kalfus studio and Shatto Recreation Center—one of reductive purity and the other the geometry of change—weave through his work.

What seems unique to Ehrlich's strategy is that while he is tending to complexity, he holds onto simplicity. Both are possible at the same time because the forms—his composite of materials and geometries—may be complex, but they are not overelaborated, and the overall organization of the basic parti is clear to the point of being diagrammatic. The detailing is simple without being obsessive.

Ehrlich is walking in a fragile territory that bridges the two contradictory terrains. In his buildings, complexity and simplicity keep each other in a tense, teasing, and contradictory balance.

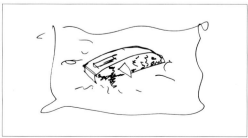

21

education ⁺ recreation

Robertson Branch Library

LOS ANGELES, CALIFORNIA
1993–1997

On Los Angeles's busy Robertson Boulevard, a civic building must compete for attention with its strip mix of traffic, billboards, and commercial buildings. The Robertson branch library, with its preweathered, copperclad "ship's hull" protruding over the sidewalk, boldly yet gracefully announces its presence on the street.

The hull pierces the library's rectangular framework like a Yankee clipper bisecting a modernist block. The gracefully curved volume is energized by being slightly skewed on all three axes, heightening the counterpoint to the grids of floor plan and elevation. The long axis is not perpendicular to the street, but points toward downtown and the main library, symbolically connecting the branch with the greater metropolis.

The 11,000-square-foot library squeezes onto a small site and concedes approximately three-quarters of the ground level to parking space. Only a multipurpose community room and administrative spaces are housed on the ground level, along with a stairway inside the vessel, which draws patrons upward. The reading room, circulation and reference desks, and public spaces are all on the second level.

In the main reading room, sloping clerestory windows, round skylights, and a peek-a-boo portal window pour natural light into the area where patrons browse or access the library's computers.

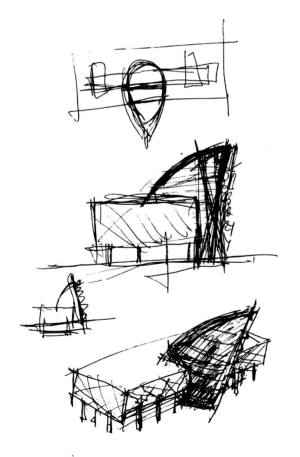

2|9|93

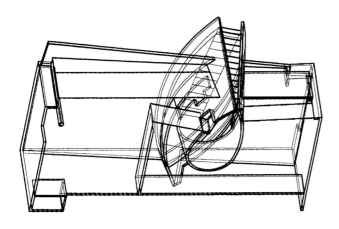

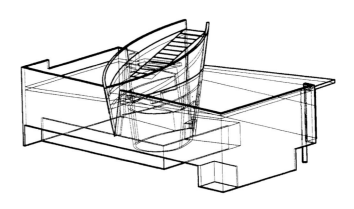

By creating a state of spatial flux with the noncoincident geometries,
    Ehrlich unlocks the usual registration of a building's coordinates, creating an indeterminate architectural condition.

— JOSEPH GIOVANNINI

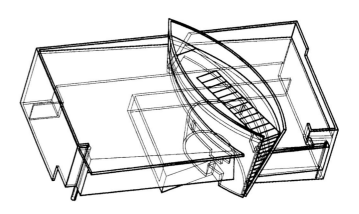

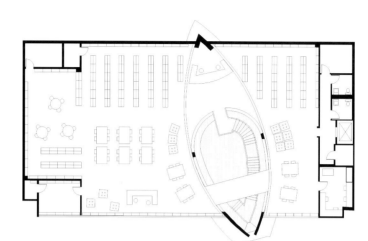

20'/6m

second floor plan

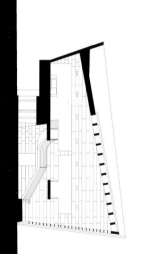

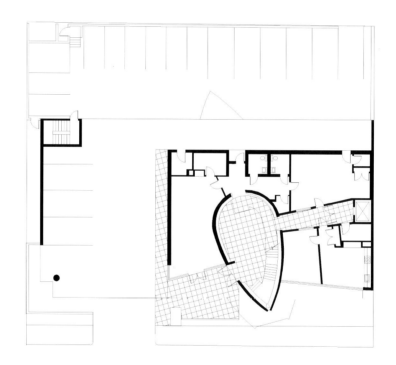

first floor plan

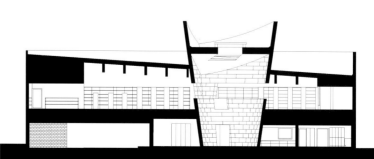

The building at once acknowledges the deconstructivist strategy of crossing two, noncoincident geometries simultaneously within the same building and cultivates the commercial vernacular within a building type normally considered institutional and cultural: Ehrlich is mixing messages as well as geometries. —JG

Child Care Center

The dramatic undulating roof of this 9,000-square-foot child care center embraces the children beneath as if to cradle them in mother's arms. The semihelix curvature results from setting the ends of the laminated wood roof beams at 6-foot intervals on a stairstep progression of steel support columns. Since the tallest columns at the front of the building are opposite the shortest in the rear, and vice versa, progressions of oppositely angled roof beams converge at the center of the structure.

Beneath the sweeping roof, the parti is simple and clear. Streetside, a nearly windowless masonry wall blocks off the outside world, while inside a circulation spine running the length of the building separates serving areas from the glass-enclosed classrooms for a hundred preschoolers. To the rear, the center becomes porous and classrooms open seamlessly into the enclosed play yard via sliding wood-and-glass doors. This openness, perpendicular to the prevailing breeze, allows natural cooling by cross ventilation ninety-five percent of the time. The rainbow-hued steel support columns and brightly colored glass set in the windows proclaim that this structure is for kids to have fun. Artist John Okulick's brightly painted steel gates, set in a stucco wall, present a welcoming face to the street, while discreetly providing security.

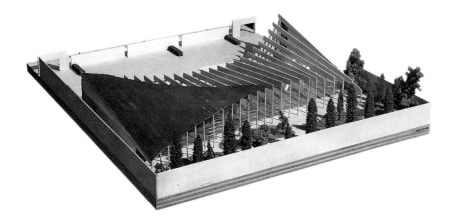

Between the convex walls and waving roof forms, the space constantly changes.

Ehrlich underscores the metamorphosing geometric character of the space decoratively: a long colonnade of pipe columns is painted in the chromatic gradient of the rainbow, and colored-glass windows waft over the back windows like clouds of free-form color. — JG

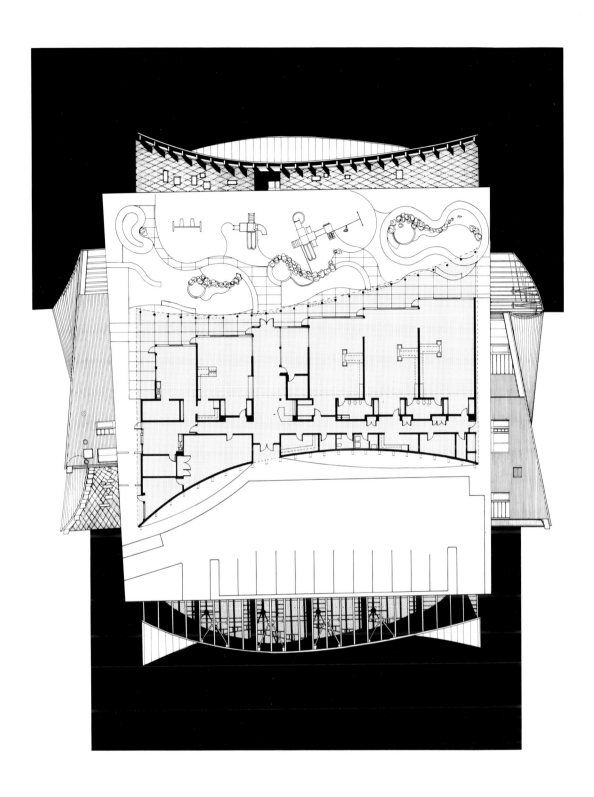

─ ─ ─ ─┤ 20'/6m   ⊝

This nursery school is simultaneously energetic and serene.
The combination makes kids happy. —STEVEN EHRLICH

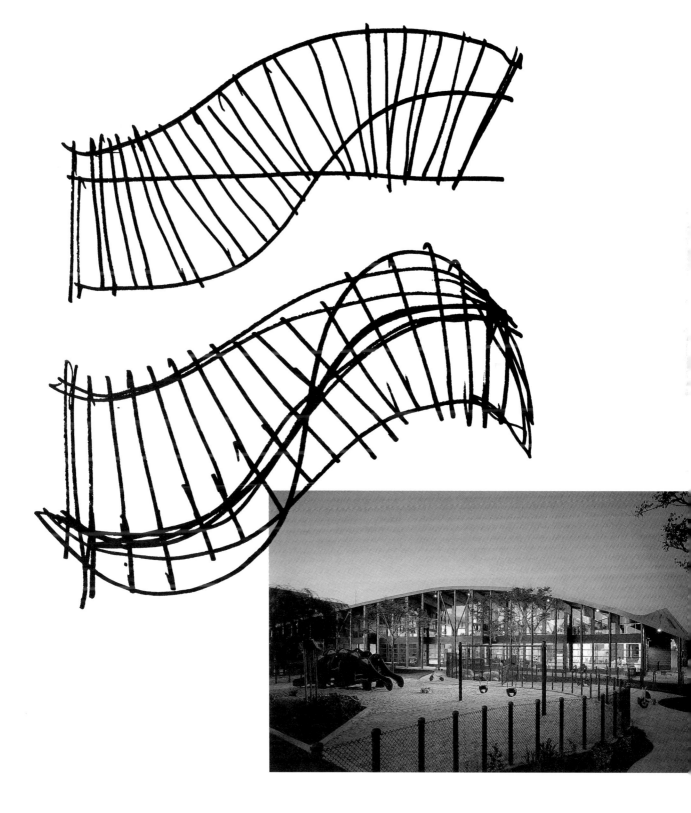

BUS **Wellness Center**

The BUS Wellness Center is an adaptive reuse of a building with "good bones"—an old Greyhound bus station converted to a facility for health and fitness training. Previous remodeling had bowdlerized the exterior of the 5,000-square-foot brick shell, but examination revealed a sound structure, including a beautiful 1950s steel, tapered girder roof frame. The original 1950s street facade was restored to reveal the roof frame and modernized with color accents and galvanized steel. The center was named BUS to save the soaring neon sign—a slice of Santa Monica history.

A central space was carved out of the interior to allow entry from both Fifth Street and the old bus parking area behind the center. This room houses the check-in area, a juice bar, and a retail sales area. Architectural forms direct patrons into a personalized weight lifting training area, an exercise and dance room, and the locker and shower facilities.

The conversion preserved existing building materials wherever possible: brick walls were sandblasted, steel framing repainted, terrazzo flooring retained. Where this wasn't possible, colored replacement materials became the solution. For example, dyed concrete sections replace the floor where it was removed to install new plumbing and wiring.

An episodic collage of mixed materials emerges, telling a tale of transformation: the original dilated space and brick walls of a bare-bones 1950s-vintage bus station acquires a denser character as Ehrlich and Seierup expose existing tapered steel girders and build interior garage doors into walls surfaced in particle board and galvanized steel.

— JG

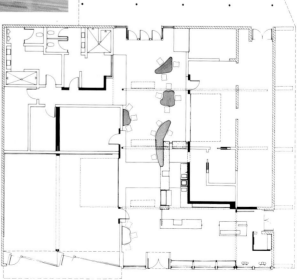

20'/6m   plan

Paul Cummins Library

The heart of the Crossroads Middle and Secondary School is a private alley that doubles as a parking lot and the "campus quad." The two-story periodical reading room of the new Paul Cummins Library protrudes into the alley, a popular student gathering spot, symbolizing the library's importance to the school and inviting students inside. A steel canopy offers a spot of shade and leads into the double-height entry volume.

About half the ground floor is dedicated to three classrooms that serve an adjacent math center. The remaining space fronts the alley and serves as the building's entry and meeting area, circulation department, and informal reading lounge. An open stair and mezzanine beckon students to the second level, which houses the library proper.

Book stacks and administrative support facilities are positioned under flanking low roofs that serve the reading and study areas, which are centrally located within a two-story-high volume. North-facing clerestory windows provide natural reading light during the day, thereby saving energy.

The 12,000-square-foot library is contained by a series of folded planes of exterior blue plaster, which descend in elevation from a peak at the building's rear elevation to the pedestrian alley front. Exposed steel framing, painted a vibrant yellow, supports the structure and inclined wall.

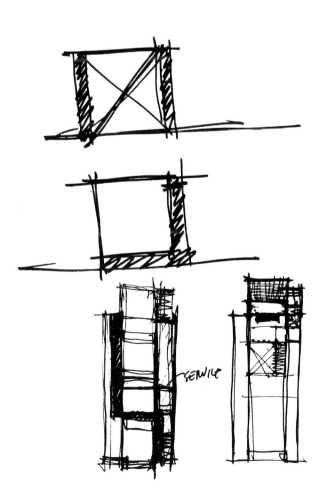

The entire space of the building, inside and out, then, is energized by leaning walls set off against an otherwise orthogonal geometry. The whole structure is conventionally built, but the slight shifts quietly radicalize form and space, sending them into dynamic equilibrium. — JG

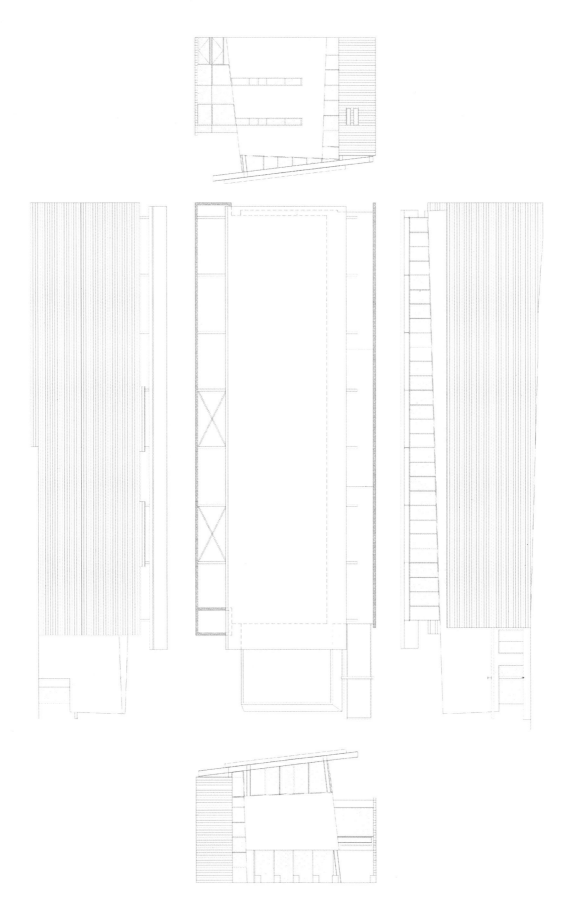

elevations and roof plan

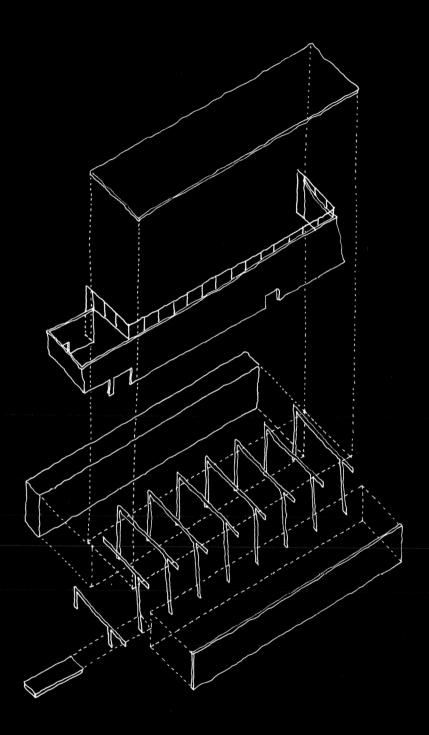

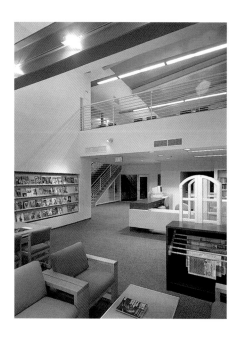

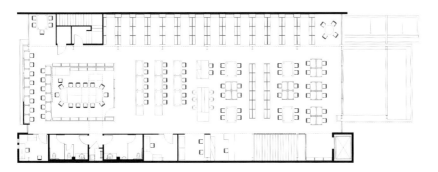

second floor plan

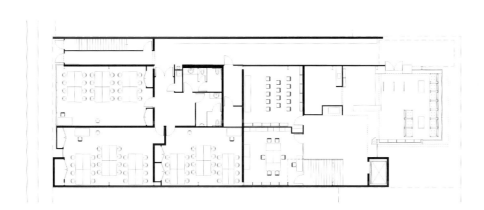
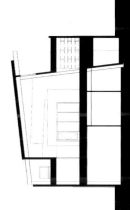

first floor plan

　20'/6m

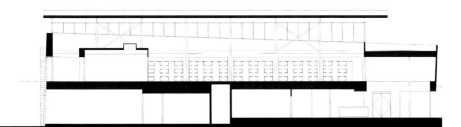

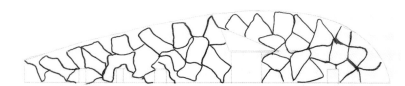

Shatto Recreation Center

This structure, with its playful, whalelike profile, marks a departure from the architect's previous work in Southern California, revealing for the first time the powerful influence of the giant mud mosques in West Africa. Shatto's organic, curved cross section and vivid colors bespeak a more intuitive, emotional origin than the restrained minimalism of the Kalfus studio (p. 184) or the Broadway Deli (p. 178).

Like the Ahmadu Bello University Theater (p. 68), this building proclaims through its primal spirit its roots in art. In the midst of a rectilinear urban setting, the accelerating and decelerating curves of the Shatto Center's roofline surprise the eye and bring a softness to its inner-city neighborhood. Flowing patterns are integral to the exterior walls, which are constructed of colored and textured structural brick and concrete block. The patterns, designed in collaboration with artist Ed Moses, reaffirm the power of art to invigorate the cityscape.

Located in a tough inner-city neighborhood, the 12,000-square-foot Shatto Center was designed to forestall vandalism and graffiti without appearing to be an urban fortress. The ethnically mixed community has embraced the building as an artistic landmark, ensuring that the Center suffered no damage during Los Angeles's 1992 riots. It remains graffiti-free to this day.

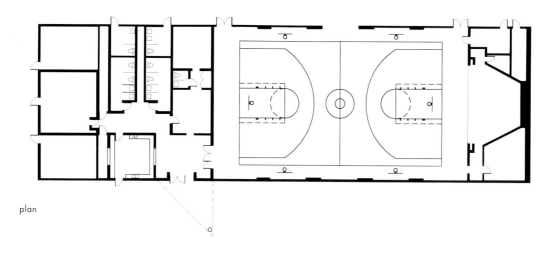

plan

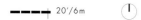 20'/6m

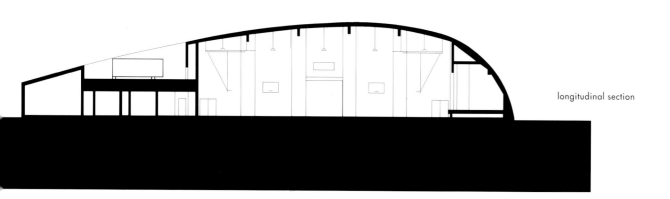

longitudinal section

Ehrlich opened the design by integrating an artist's energy, insight, and insolence, invigorating what is all too often a closed and stiff architectural process with the artist's gestural spontaneity. — JG

If the Kalfus studio of the early 1980s represents one design paradigm,
Ehrlich finds another some five years later, as represented by the Shatto Recreation Center.

The premise of its design was a radical departure. — JG

SHATTO
RECREATION CENTER
COMMUNITY BUILDING
3101

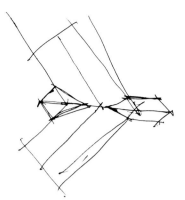

TOKYO, JAPAN
1985–1986

Futiko-Tamagowon Reception Center

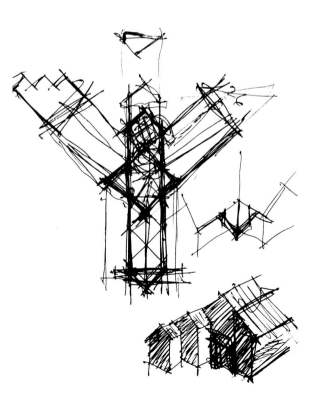

Gables and roof planes rise and peak like the wings of an origami bird. This 4,000-square-foot multipurpose building, which serves as the reception center, showroom, and gallery for an ongoing Tokyo housing exposition, explores the tension between western and Japanese architectural concepts.

The major Japanese home builders who commissioned the project, for which Yamada & Associates served as executive architects, sought a future-oriented demonstration house to provide space for exhibits, meetings, and seminars. The two arms of the y-shaped design accommodate these needs, while the central axis of the house merges tradition with innovation.

Visitors proceed through a galleria evoking the traditional Japanese *tori*, or spiritual pathway, executed in precast concrete columns and lintels. This processional entrance hall culminates at a sunken home office center, with windows looking out on a sculpture by Guy Dill in the garden. The building's exterior skin of reflective glass and steel reinterprets the Japanese tradition of wall and garden by mirroring trees, rocks, and sculpture.

炭屋旅館 京都市中京区麩屋町三条下ル
電話（221）2180・2187〜9 ☎604

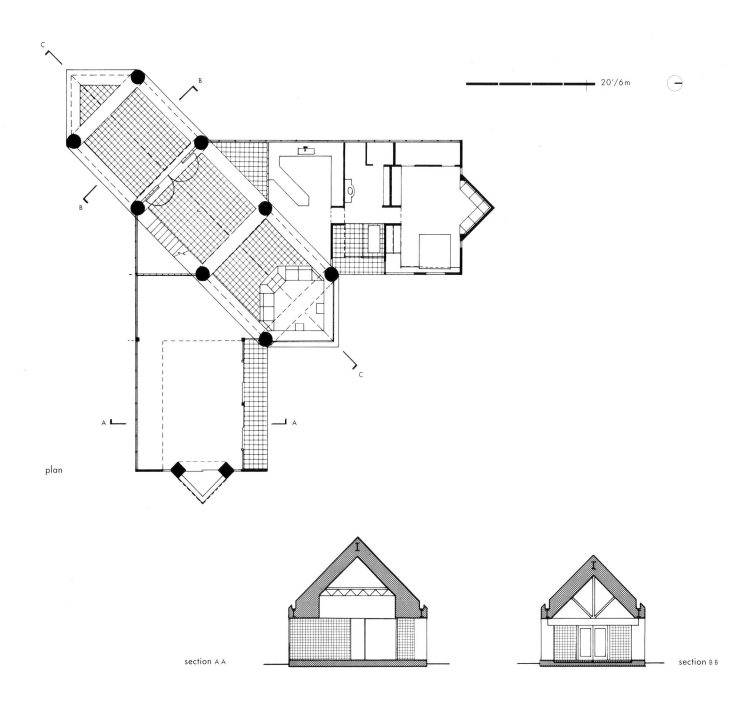

plan

20'/6m

section A A

section B B

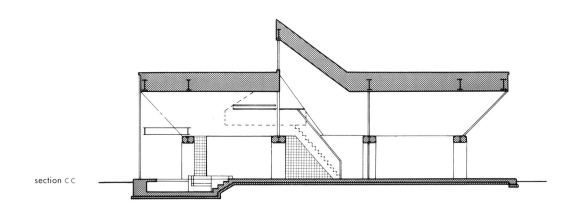

section C C

This design straddles the Japan–Los Angeles cultural border.
It meets the Japanese clients' expectations of a California architect and my desire to interpret Japan through
a broad definition of vernacular modernism. — SE

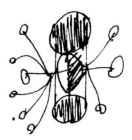

Ahmadu Bello University Theater

Innovation enriches, rather than diminishes, tradition in this African university theater. Earthen walls express the continent's ancient ties to the soil. Yet theaters—buildings dedicated exclusively to drama and performance—were not among pre-European Africa's architectural inventory.

In plan the theater resembles the mud-walled compound houses of Nigeria's Hausa cities. But the design reinterprets the vernacular round huts and square *soro* rooms of the indigenous architectural tradition. For example, the round roof spans far exceed traditional scale, and the doorways to the *soros* are placed at the corner, not in a side wall, as is customary. Local artisans decorated the walls of the entrance *soro* with a form of bas relief that is falling rapidly into disuse. The design on the back of the *soro* evokes an African mask.

The theater's circular central performance area and the smaller spaces provided by the four huts permit many staging arrangements—from the standard proscenium stage to theater-in-the-round. This fusion of flexible function with traditional forms fits the theater department's goal of producing new forms of African drama.

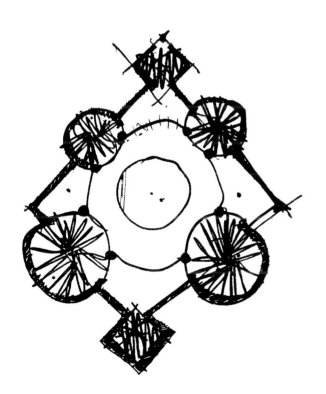

My interest in integrating art and architecture commenced on this project.
By collaborating with the finest family of bas-relief artists in Zaria,
we brought in centuries of cultural identity through their art. — SE

20'/6m

People sit on woven mats or moveable chairs.
The student performers define the space through their own creative staging,

which is encouraged by the theater's flexibility. — SE

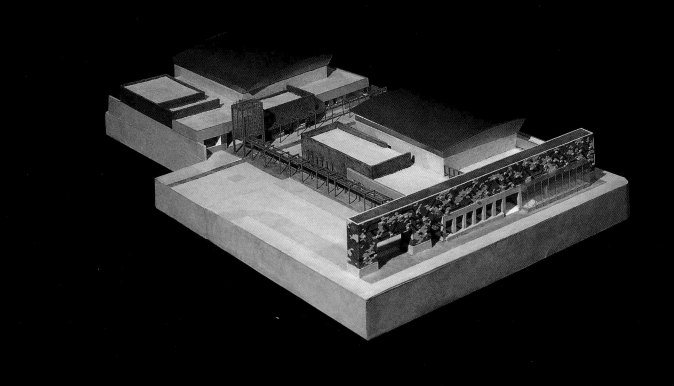

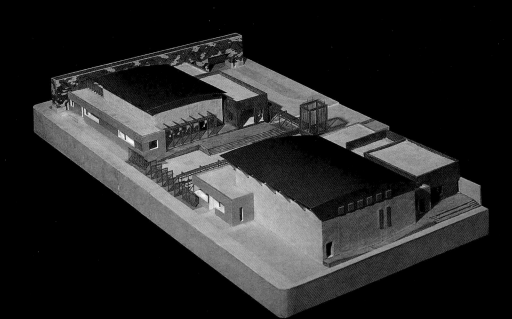

Biblioteca Latinoamericana and Washington Area Youth Center

THE REDEVELOPMENT AGENCY OF
THE CITY OF SAN JOSE
SAN JOSE, CALIFORNIA
1996–1999

The 15,000-square-foot library and 17,000-square-foot youth center form an integrated, landscaped complex designed to become a magnet for activities in the surrounding community and also serve as a dramatic urban landmark. Garcia Teague Architecture & Interiors are the executive architects for the project.

The complex presents a symbolic face to the city in the form of a massive, patterned wall fronting First Street, a major traffic arterial leading from San Jose's burgeoning suburbs to downtown. The monumentally scaled concrete, masonry, and brick wall serves as a highly abstracted artwork. Its face consists of a recurring, historical Latin American design motif interwoven with modern, abstract patterns rooted in modern art—a combination hinting at San Jose's high-tech future and its rich Latino history.

The shaded courtyard between the two buildings, with its permanent raised stage, creates a plaza-like public space for fiestas, an amenity now lacking in the neighborhood. Two shaded pedestrian corridors reach like open arms from the courtyard to First and Oak streets, and invite visitors.

The library and youth center are united in their formal relationship and share a common material vocabulary. Each structure consists of three tall masonry masses that are unified by one-story elements painted bright yellow. The tallest volumes form the central space of each building, with vaulted roofs and clerestory windows.

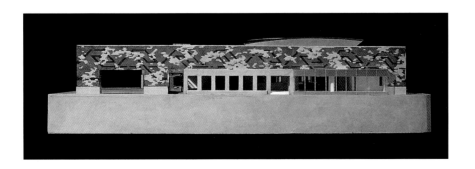

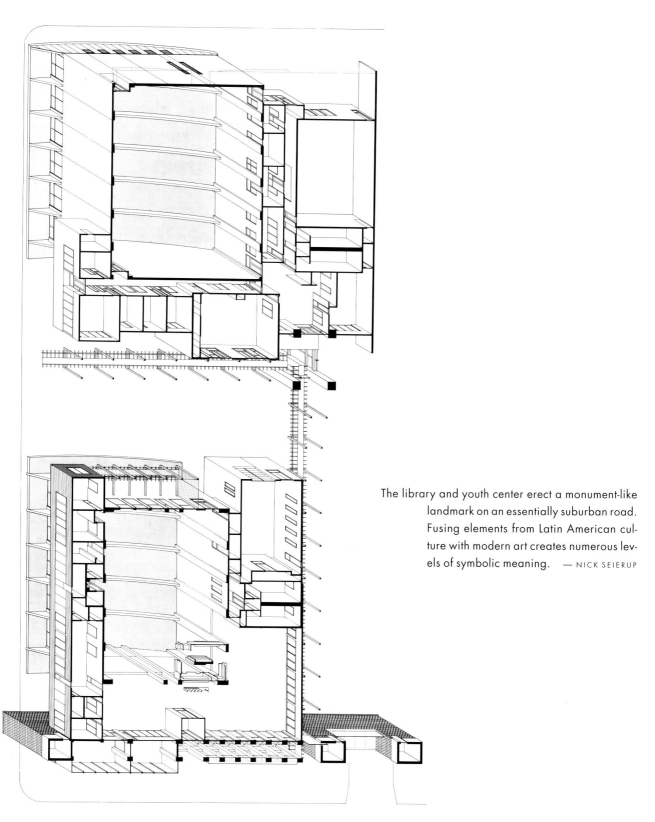

The library and youth center erect a monument-like landmark on an essentially suburban road. Fusing elements from Latin American culture with modern art creates numerous levels of symbolic meaning. — NICK SEIERUP

worm's-eye axonometric

bird's-eye axonometric

habitation

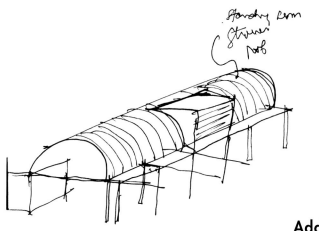

Standing Rom Stivner Norb

Addition to
Neutra Beach House

CYCLOIDAL VAULTS

The 1938 Lewin house designed by Richard Neutra rests at the base of a Santa Monica bluff overlooking the Pacific Ocean. The present owners purchased the adjoining lot to build a complementary 3,400-square-foot addition consisting of an entertainment pavilion and pool, additional garage and parking areas, and servants' and guests' quarters.

The new garage and servants' living area were positioned to form a barrier to the nearby Pacific Coast Highway. This plan created a courtyard with the original Neutra house as a backdrop. A glass bridge links the house with the new entertainment pavilion, which is roofed with a stainless steel, cycloidal arch reminiscent of Louis Kahn's Kimball Art Museum. Echoing Neutra's vision of fusing interior and exterior, three walls of the 16-foot-wide pavilion consist of floor-to-ceiling glass. Glass doors slide completely away into wall pockets. Pavilion, garage, and servants' quarters are terminated on the side away from the house by serving elements. These elements are housed in cast-in-place concrete.

The Pacific, framed by a large opening in the compound wall, becomes the termination of a strong visual axis that aligns the pool and the entertainment pavilion with the dramatic ocean view.

The first decision was not to replicate Neutra's late-1930s architecture, but to take cues from it. The dialogue between each piece, old and new, energizes both. — SE

20'/6m

first floor plan

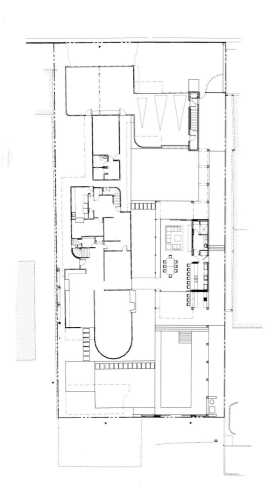

second floor plan

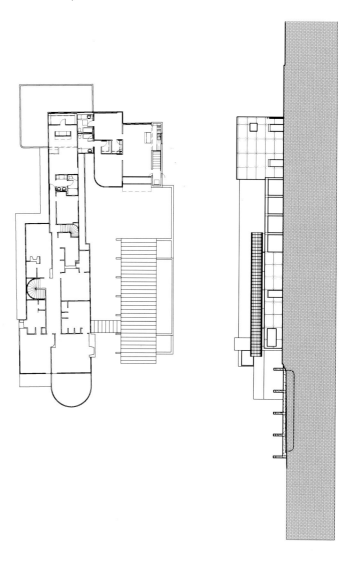

west elevation

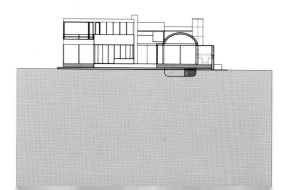

east elevation

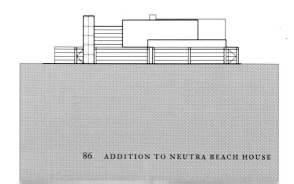

86   ADDITION TO NEUTRA BEACH HOUSE

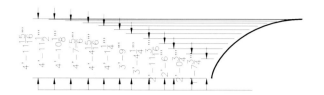

mathematical formulation of cycloidal arch

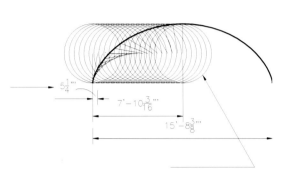

$5\frac{1}{4}'''$

$7'-10\frac{3}{16}'''$

$15'-8\frac{3}{8}'''$

Schulman House

The Schulman house marks a critical evolutionary step in the architect's treatment of cubic masses. The 1981 Kalfus studio (p. 184) stands as an austere expression of cubist modernism. The later Miller-Nazarey (p. 138) and Gold-Friedman (p. 122) houses embody more fragmented cubic volumes, spaces in complex interaction with each other and the surrounding environment. The Schulman house adds sophisticated use of natural materials, such as copper and wood, which add a warmth not associated with modernism.

Offsetting one wing of the house by 17 degrees, to conform to the curve of the surrounding canyon wall, dramatically energizes the symmetrical order of the H-shaped parti. This asymmetry is expanded by extending the offset wing to address programmatic requirements. The legs of the irregular H form a sheltered forecourt, landscaped with Zen restraint, which provides a serene, Japanese-inspired prelude to entering the house.

The entryway slices between two cast-in-place concrete walls, each enclosing a stairway. Once inside, the visitor passes beneath an interior bridge connecting the two-story wings to emerge into a 20-foot-high explosion of light and space. The extensive use of wood and burnished copper detailing broadens the palette of materials and foreshadows the more intricate elaboration of cubic volumes of the later Benenson house (p. 146).

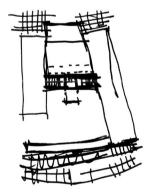

site plan

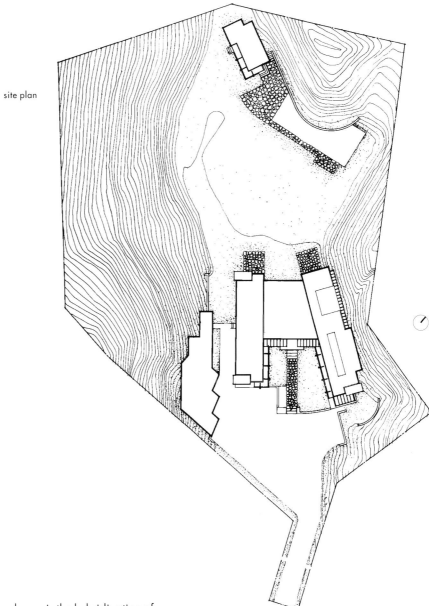

■━━┥ 20'/6m

The important advance in the Schulman house is the hybridization of
three materials and building vocabularies; the composite
of concrete, stucco, and wood represents a juxtaposition of
machine-tooled abstraction and craft traditions. — JG

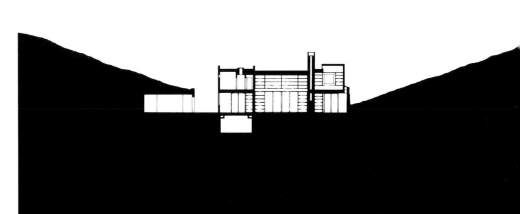

site section

section looking north

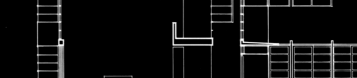

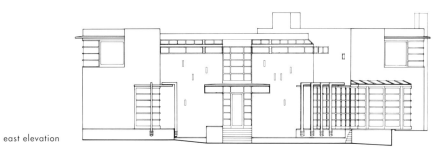

east elevation

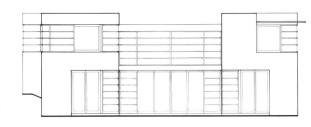

west elevation

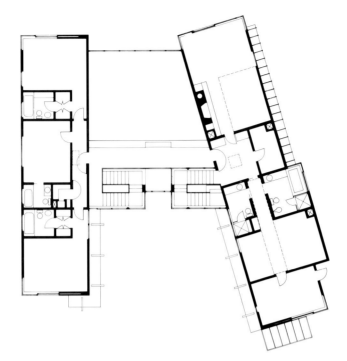

second floor plan

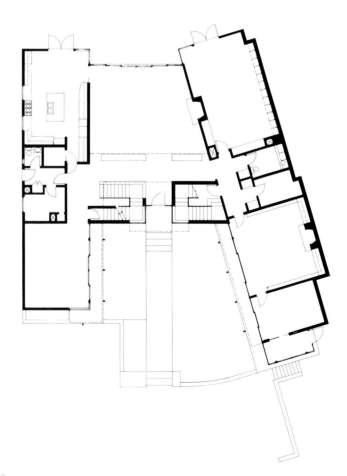

first floor plan

20'/6m

The barrier between indoors and outdoors dissolves as the rooms orient to the outside,
as though in a state of architectural meditation. — JG

The Farrell house appears to be a new construction, but in reality is a radical renovation of a typical 1950s California tract bungalow.

Farrell House

The building's footprint is a straightforward rectangular box cut away to incorporate an existing lap pool. In section, however, the most prominent feature is a two-story barrel vault that runs the length of the structure. Box-like stucco volumes, painted purple and ocher, serve as counterpoints to the main sculptural form, whose roof and exterior walls are painted black. The foundation and two existing bedrooms were retained from the original house.

Redesigned for a rock musician, the 2,200-square-foot house celebrates southern California's year-round benign climate, with the lap pool becoming the focus of the new design. Facing the pool on the south facade, a glass wall slides completely away into a wall pocket to remove the barrier between interior and exterior. Large sliding glass doors in other rooms open to courtyards and a roof terrace, further erasing the boundaries between inside and out.

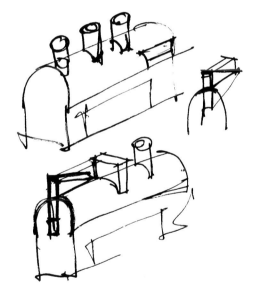

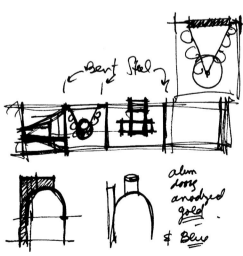

site plan

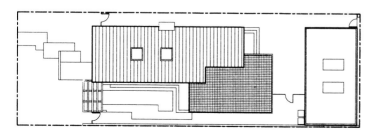

20'/6m

The owner embraced non-Western cultural influences, resulting in the dining room table having a built-in Korean barbecue replete with a Japanese-influenced surrounding wood seating pit. — SE

second floor plan

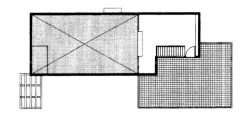

——————— 20'/6m

first floor plan

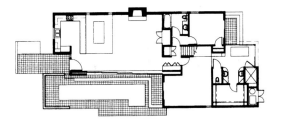

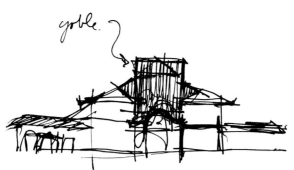

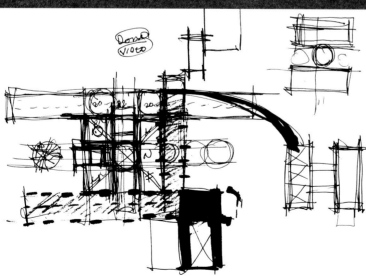

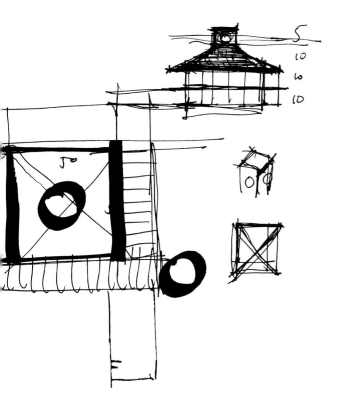

Lo House

The clients, a Taiwanese family recently settled in the United States, sought a design to fuse their Chinese heritage with a modern California vernacular. Chinese masters of *feng shui*, an ancient wisdom for balancing forces, played a role in locating the home on the site and in other design decisions, such as orienting the front door toward the south.

The underlying order is based upon a traditional *feng shui* matrix called *bugua*, represented by a nine-cell grid. The nine cells are grouped in the parti as two two-story wings with canted walls, which flank and are parallel to a central atrium. In the atrium, fourteen 10-inch-thick columns soar 32 feet to the ceiling, supporting wooden corbels influenced by pagoda detailing. The canted-wall wings contain bedrooms on the second floor. At the rear of the house, a separate wing perpendicular to the living room axis contains auxiliary serving elements.

The architecture of the exterior is an abstracted reinterpretation of traditional Chinese temple form, massing, and proportion. The traditional articulated stone base, canted walls, deep eaves, and massive sheltering roof are fused with a modern materials palette of polished concrete block, burnished plaster, and roll-up glass doors.

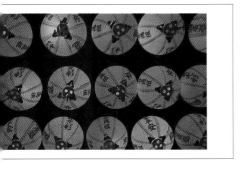

Traditional Chinese lanterns

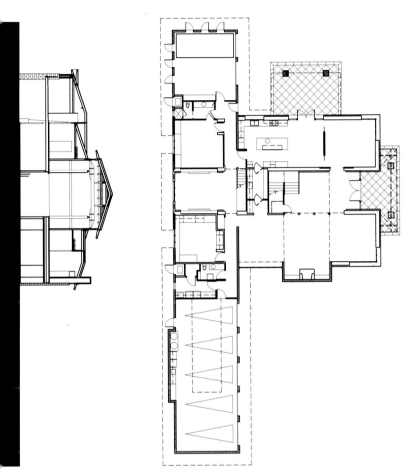

first floor plan

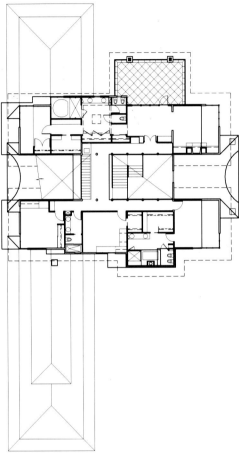

second floor plan

20'/6m

Both architect and *feng shui* master listened to and accommodated each other,
demonstrating that the world is becoming a global community. — SE

west elevation

north elevation

south elevation

east elevation

Douroux House

Venice, California, like its eponymous Italian counterpart, boasts picturesque canals. The building site, directly fronting the intersection of two of Venice's recently restored waterways, offers prime scenic vistas. However, a small lot and a 25-foot building height limit called for an innovative design to take advantage of the sunny waterside location.

The solution lay in compactly stacking secondary programmatic spaces into three stories at the rear of the lot, adjacent to an alley. Fronting the water, the ground-level living room has a 16-foot-high glass wall along the canal, while its roof forms the platform for an elevated garden adjoining the master suite. The tiered design of the 3,700-square-foot house maximizes exposure to sun, sky, and canal views, while editing out the dense urban environment to the sides and rear.

Automobile access is via the alley. The rear wall of this three-story residential and service tower turns a blank face to the noise and traffic of the alley, but admits light through frosted glass.

The difficult puzzle of a tight site on a Venice canal is solved by maximizing the floor area on the alley side. — SE

canal elevation   alley elevation

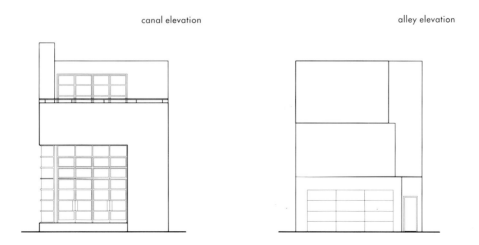

third floor plan

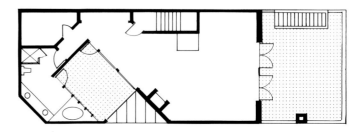

second floor plan

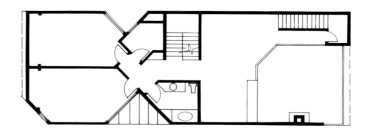

first floor plan

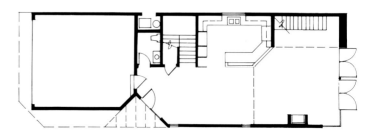

longitudinal section

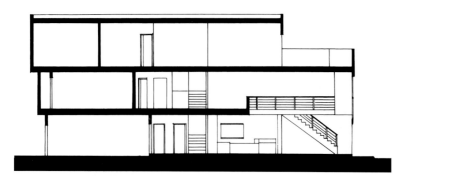

20'/6m

Gold-Friedman House

This house in the Santa Monica canyon creates a hillside courtyard with the rear of the structure engaging a steep canyon wall in a multilevel dialogue. The recess between the canyon wall and the rear of the house becomes an outdoor garden room, its boundaries edged in stair-stepped retainers. A bridge leaps from the house to the terraced hillside beyond. This dialogue between residence and hillside reinforces the connection of the house to its natural setting while at the same time expanding and elaborating the courtyard concept in an urban context.

The bedrooms are located, in conventional fashion, above the public areas. About 1,500 of the house's total 5,000 square feet are located in the split-level, subterranean basement. This area includes the service portions of the house and forms a pedestal for the principal spaces. A split-level stairway forms the central spine, vertically partitioning the structure. A stair-stepped skylight with frosted horizontal and clear vertical glass panes illuminates the stairwell.

The public facade of the house presents a fragmented, cubist face to the world, with plants hanging from horizontal edges. A multiplatform stairway leading to a broad front porch elaborates the complex interplay with the street.

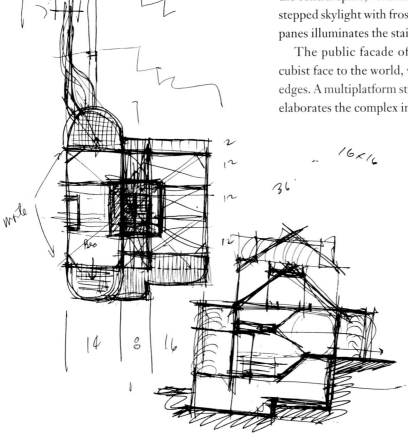

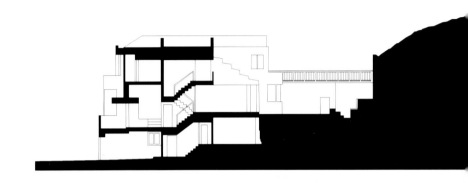

In the Gold-Friedman house,
   Ehrlich breaks up the three-story masses into highly plastic compositions of asymmetrically cubic volumes
   that recede and advance as the house steps up the hillside slope. — JG

first floor plan

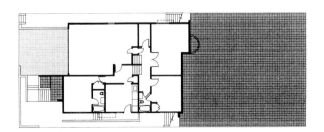

second floor plan

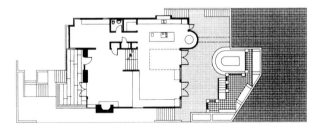

third floor plan

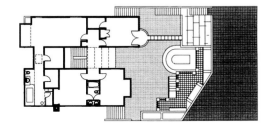

20'/6m

Hempstead House

Repeated squares and rectangles define the plan, elevations, and interior detailing of this 2,000-square-foot Venice house. The characteristic integration of interior and exterior is achieved by treating patio and pool as extensions of the living room, the culmination of a visual corridor extending from the front door, through the living room, and to the rear wall past the pool's end. Extensive windows, skylights, and glass doors flood the interior with light. As if to counter this openness and temper the Southern California sun, however, the design features deeply recessed windows and doors set in walls as thick as 3 feet.

The owner, a television and film director, worked closely with Ehrlich to develop the earthy, organic scheme of color and natural materials. The burnt sienna and yellow ocher of the exterior, used to detail the mantels of living room and bedroom fireplaces, suffuse the interior with warm bursts of color.

site plan

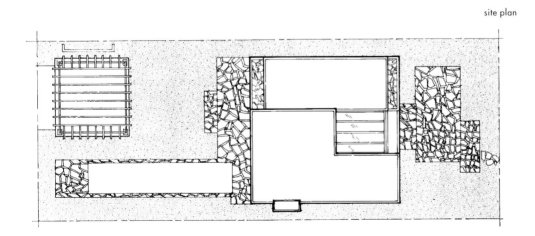

20'/6m

As the owner and I contemplated a beautiful ceramic cup hand-painted in Italy,
the color scheme for the house emerged. — SE

section and plans

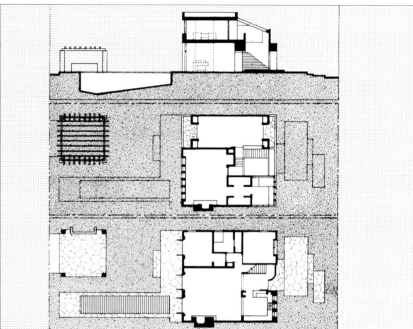

20'/6m

Miller-Nazarey House

The 4,500-square-foot Miller-Nazarey residence, situated on the edge of a canyon, forsakes sweeping views for more intimate, private vistas. The living room opens onto an outdoor garden and courtyard pool. Shoji screens and sliding glass doors permit endless variations on sky, sun, and shadow. The shoji and glass doors disappear into the walls, dissolving at a touch the boundaries between indoors and out.

The three-story atrium provides a ceremonial entrance to the house; a "column of sound" from the slender waterfall near the door cleanses entrants of the traffic, noise, and distractions of the outside world. The atrium, which divides the house in two, floods adjacent rooms with light from its 12' x 18' skylight. Within the atrium's massive enclosed space, steel structural elements harmonize with the glass brick walls to express an airy lightness. Glass and vierendeel-truss steel bridges, crossing the atrium, link the two sides of the house with transparent aerial pathways.

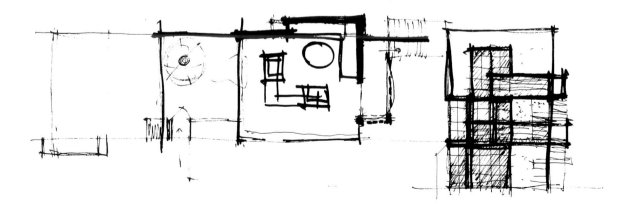

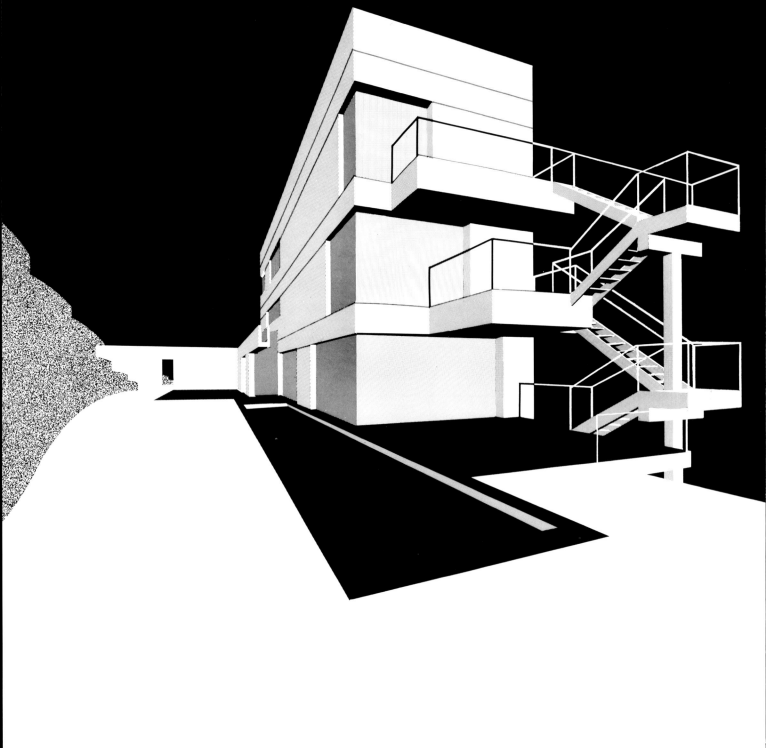

Walking across the glass bridges creates the feeling of being
suspended in space. — SE

The Miller-Nazarey house can be closed by either a set of sliding glass doors or shoji screens, or left completely open to the domestic Eden. — JG

third floor plan

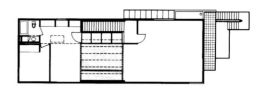

second floor plan

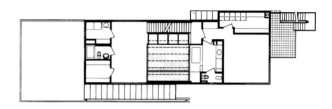

first floor plan

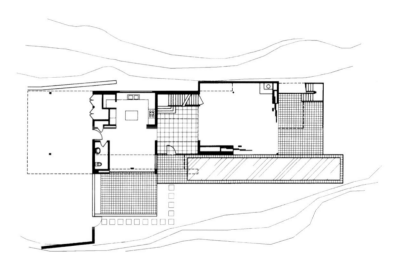

20'/6m

longitudinal section

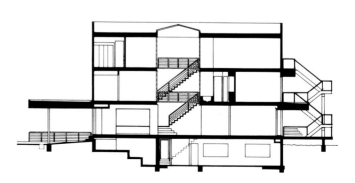

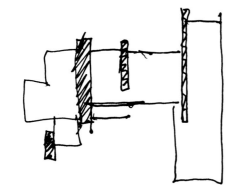

Benenson House

The handling of cubic volumes in the 7,500-square-foot Benenson house marks the latest stage in a gradual evolution that began with the pure, modernist expression of the Kalfus studio (p. 184) and evolved into the opened corners of the Miller-Nazerey house (p. 138) and the elaborated integration of architectural vocabularies and building materials of the Schulman house (p. 92). The Benenson house extends this progression by integrating colored, elongated cubes as major design elements. These burnished stucco volumes not only house serving elements such as fireplaces, stairs, mechanical cores, and storage; they also cascade through the house, producing a dynamic vertical rhythm of form and color.

A series of cascading copper-clad horizontal canopies serve as a counterpoint to these elongated masses. They protect natural wood, glass windows, and doors from rain and sun, adding a horizontal balance of floating planes in a Mondrianesque composition of forms. The ever changing two-story composition of vertical and horizontal planes steps down the hillside, dynamically engaging indoor spaces with the verdant canyon setting.

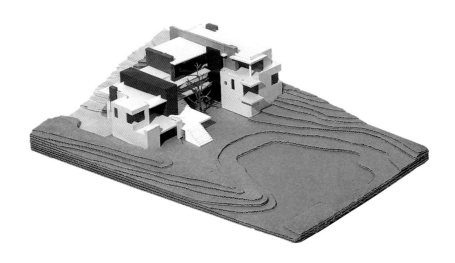

Some of the cubic forms interrupting the building's mass are thin enough to seem like Mondrianesque lines cast in syncopated boogie-woogie rhythms: Ehrlich liberates the house into a play of form by bringing the asymmetrical disposition of cubic volumes into the de Stijl–like composition. — JG

vertical cubic forms

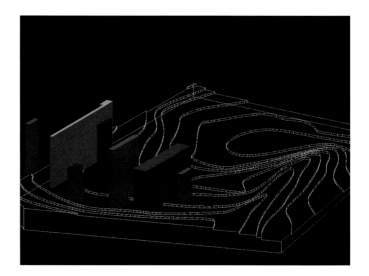

+ horizontal planes

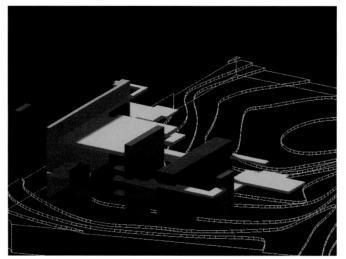

+ cubic mass

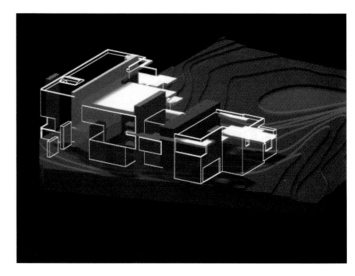

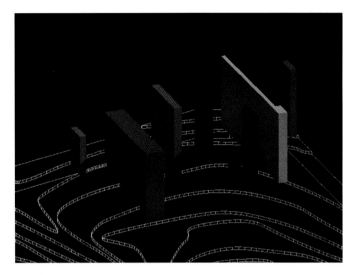

vertical cubic forms

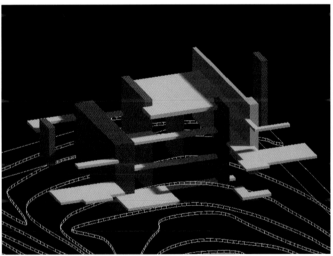

+ horizontal planes

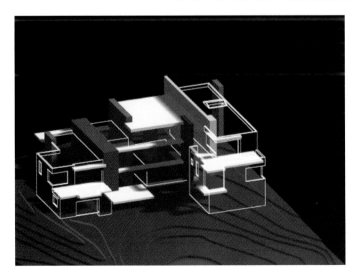

+ cubic mass

The cubes are not simply visually strong: they become agents breaking up the mass of the house; volumes start slipping with planes to the outside, pushing parts into and out of the yard, like forces. — JG

north elevation

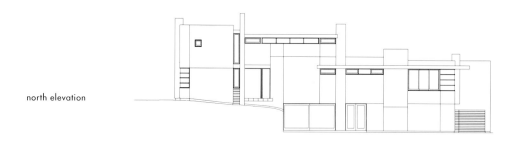

south elevation

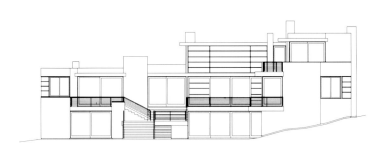

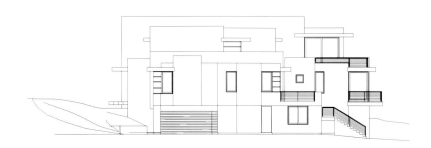

west elevation

east elevation

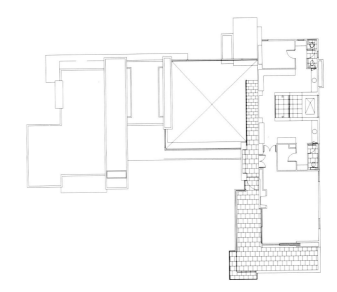

third floor plan

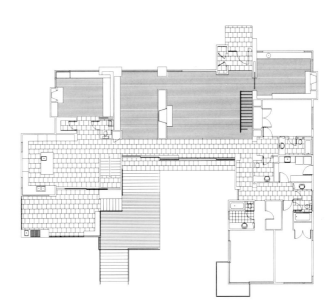

second floor plan

 20'/6m

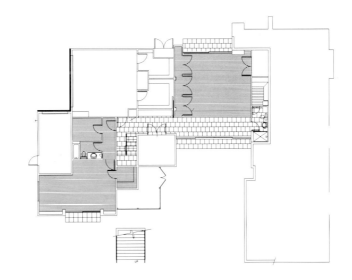

first floor plan

arts and communication

DreamWorks SKG Animation Studios

The DreamWorks SKG Animation Studios is the most advanced studio facility constructed in the Hollywood area. It integrates modern construction methods with the massive digital and fiber optic infrastructure needed to "wire" a complex dedicated to advanced computerized film animation—all laid out in a scheme echoing historical southern European city plans.

Occupying a 13-acre triangular site next to the Los Angeles River, the 320,000-square-foot studios (expanding to nearly 500,000 square feet in Phase II of the project) create the combination "high tech, high touch" environment needed for a creative corps of more than a thousand employees. The Gensler firm is the executive architect for the project.

Elaborating on the courtyard scheme of the Sony Music Entertainment campus (p. 170), the Animation Studio complex is organized as a hierarchy of open spaces, providing locations for open-air meetings and encounters. At the heart of the complex lies a large common plaza, or "piazza." Each of the five buildings possesses its own courtyard, all of which spill onto the piazza or the man-made river that traces the vestigial path where the Los Angeles River once ran through the site.

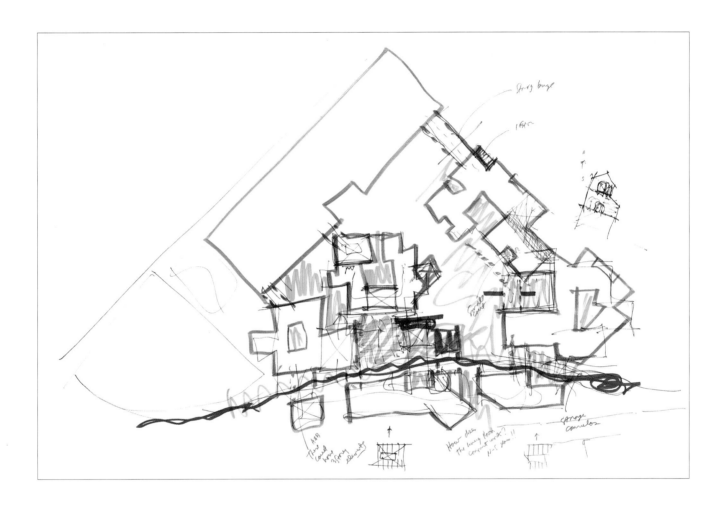

The way-finding is done through the hierarchy of outdoor spaces. Given the anomie of the car-oriented streets of Los Angeles, Ehrlich uses the courtyards as a way of creating and intensifying a sense of community. — JG

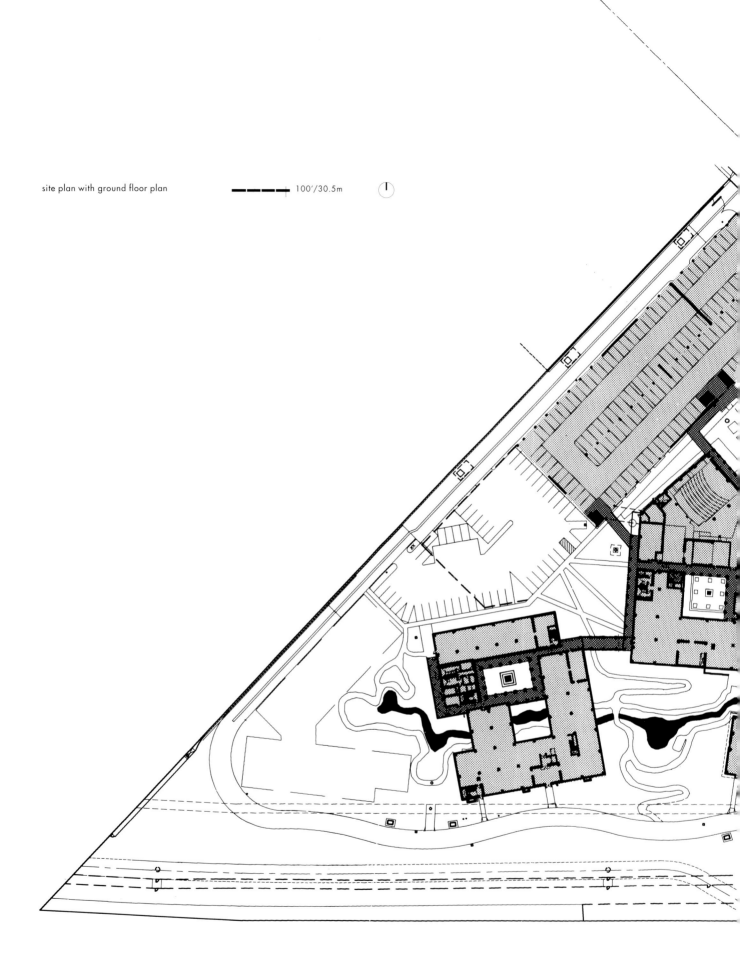

site plan with ground floor plan

100'/30.5m

SONY PICTURES ENTERTAINMENT
CULVER CITY, CALIFORNIA
1992–1994

Bow Truss Studio

The Bow Truss Studio is an adaptive reuse of a 1930s red brick industrial building. Its crown is a wood-arched bow truss roof, newly elevated above the brick walls by a clerestory. The reworked low-tech structure now houses the high-tech video studio used to produce Sony's Game Show Network television shows.

The building is conceived as a grouping of internal spaces surrounding a central gallery. Natural light floods into this two-story gallery via the new clerestory light monitor, which is supported by six large steel columns angled to match the imaginary, extended radius lines defining the curve of the bow truss roof. A second floor, independently supported by its own structural system, has been added.

Principal spaces in the 15,000-square-foot building consist of the broadcasting studio, a completely glass-enclosed conference room, and a "technical core," all adjacent to the atrium. The technical core displays its hardware behind a glazed wall near the building's main entrance and contrasts with the seeming impenetrability of the broadcasting studio.

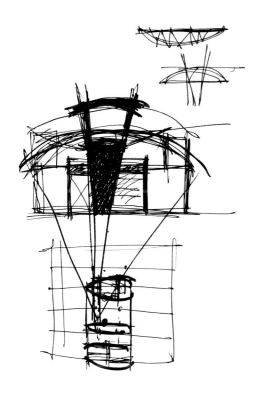

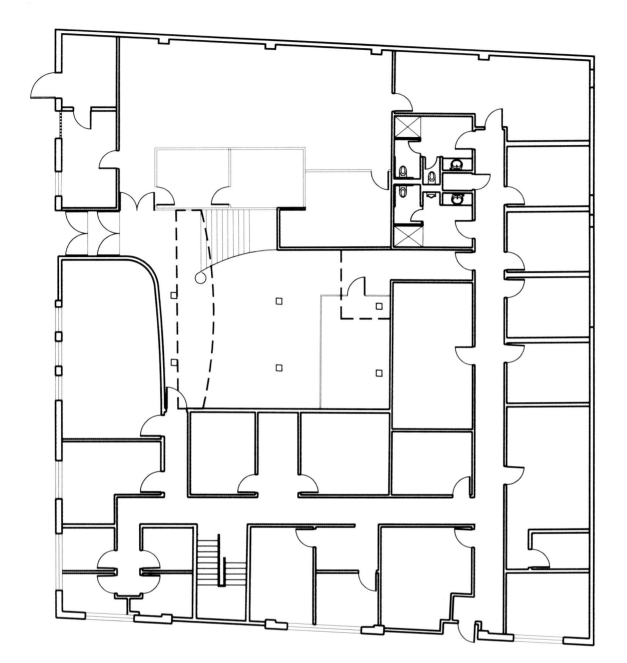

first floor plan

20'/6m

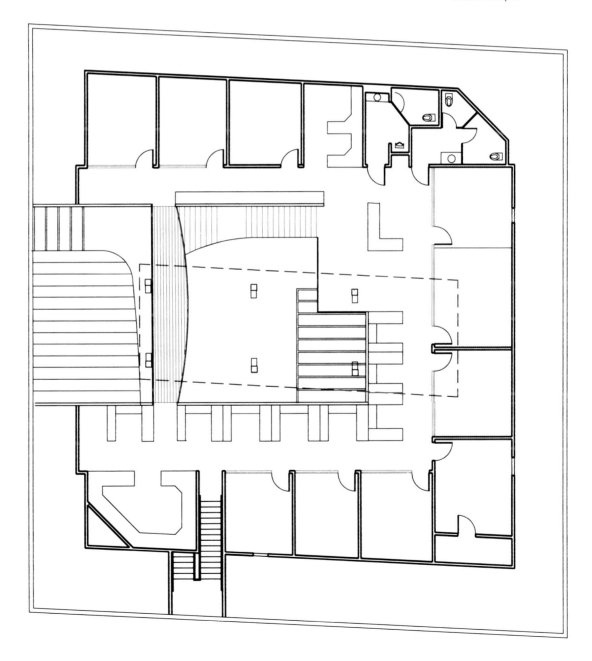

We saved a slice of Los Angeles history by "turbocharging" this 1930s industrial shell. Old and new elements complement each other to become a synergistic whole. — SE

WEST COAST HEADQUARTERS
SANTA MONICA, CALIFORNIA
1991–1992

Sony Music Entertainment

The Sony Music campus marks the architect's first elaboration of interior courtyards in a large-scale commercial project.

With its public facade, the three-building, stone-clad complex reflects an appreciation of the "streamline moderne" architecture popular in Santa Monica during the 1930s.

The complex houses Sony's two main record labels and corporate support services, including a recording studio and performance space. The lobbies of all three buildings open onto the lushly-planted and waterscaped courtyard entered through an abstractly designed gateway by artist Guy Dill. Allées and a courtyard cafe give rise to impromptu encounters.

From streetside, the visual focus of the project is the corner of Twentieth Street and Colorado Avenue, where a soaring triangular wedge counterpoints a carved stone curve, adding visual drama for quickly passing motorists. The street facades also contrast the primitive with the futuristic by juxtaposing Arizona sandstone with the gloss of polished green translucent glass.

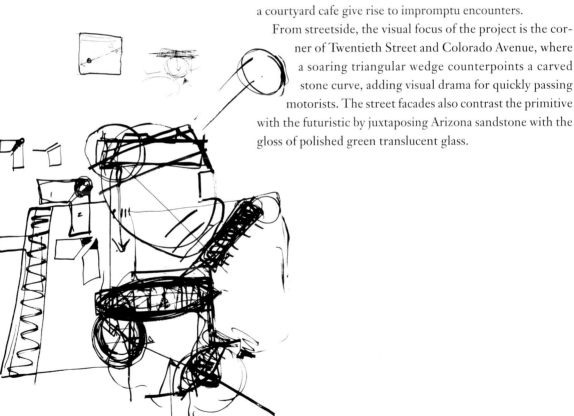

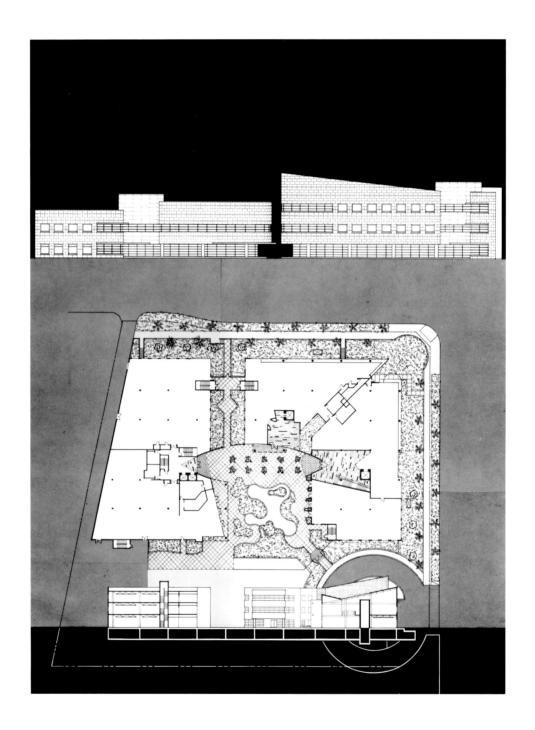

Whenever the program allows, Ehrlich creates a socializing space similar to the courtyards and squares he encountered in North Africa. These outdoor courts are especially appropriate in Southern California as spaces that collect people on their way to and from desk and parking. — JG

Broadway Deli

The Broadway Deli evokes the lively spirit of African and Asian marketplaces, where commerce and community coincide. The design for the restaurant and specialty delicatessen consists of an airy, open floor plan with exposed kitchen and bakery ovens. The bar, wine shop, market, and other businesses function as "neighborhoods," creating intimacy and focus within the larger context of the 9,000-square-foot interior.

Materials for the Broadway's interior—stainless steel, colored concrete, and dyed and natural woods—serve to reinterpret traditional New York delis and European brasseries; they also articulate the uncluttered modernist design. Lighting consists of a subtle interplay of soffit-hidden neon, recessed incandescent, and small, bright halogen bulbs dropped from the ceiling. The southern window wall floods the interior with daylight and connects patrons with the lively street scene outside, as does the sidewalk cafe on Santa Monica's busy Third Street Promenade.

The Broadway Deli has become Santa Monica's "front porch." — SE

plan

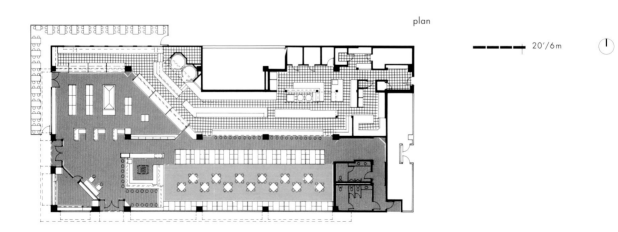

20'/6m

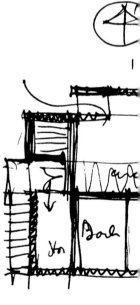

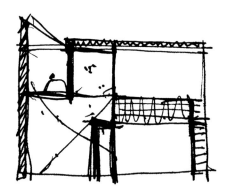

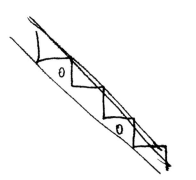

Kalfus Studio

The Kalfus studio was the architect's first freestanding built structure in Los Angeles. Attracting wide critical attention because of its uncompromising spareness, its modernist use of cubic volumes foreshadows much of the later work.

The studio heralds the beginning of the architect's experimentation with the dramatic counterpoint between a massive, primitively simple entry facade and an explosion of light and space inside, rendered through an innovative use of materials and technology. The unadorned entry elevation gives no hint of the light-splashed interior behind the door. Inside, stairstep glazing on the north wall and 14-foot-high, steel-sash factory windows on the east wall admit California light into a radiant chamber.

The use of shadow as an ornamental element—continuing in many later works—is adumbrated here. The blankly rectangular exterior entry wall lacks decoration. Yet the sun becomes an unwitting design element by casting a constantly changing shadow pattern through the grate treads of the steel stairway mounted on the wall.

The compact (1,250 square feet) Kalfus studio serves both as a guest house and photography and painting studio. Its vertically cubistic design both complements and counterpoints the horizontal openness of the adjacent Richard Neutra house, engaging the two in a modernist pas de deux.

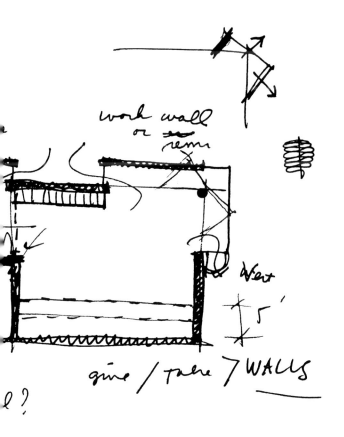

The structure is remarkable for its disciplined simplicity and purity, and for its crisp abstraction. It was conceived at a time when architects in the United States were slipping into the lavender palette and classicist vocabulary of postmodernism.

In that context, the effort was fresh and individualistic:
Ehrlich was marching to his own drum rather than to the beat of the national press based in the East. — JG

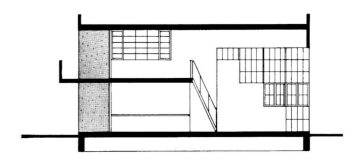

longitudinal section

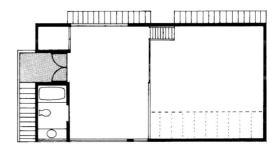

second floor plan

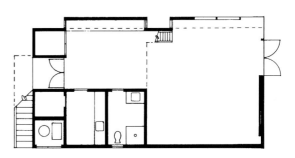

first floor plan

20'/6m

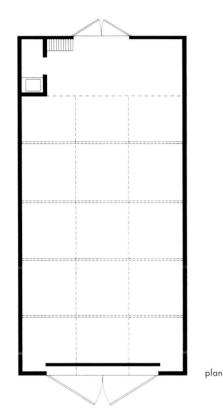

plan

Moses Studio

The rectangular interior of this studio for artist Ed Moses, with its massive, exposed trusses, evokes the craftsmanship and the dignified simplicity of a Shaker church. The 1,400-square-foot design reconciles the artist's utilitarian requirement for abundant, light-filled work space with his aesthetic need for spiritually satisfying surroundings in which to create.

Clerestory windows running the length of the cupola flood the work area with soft, ambient light. Expanses of unbroken white walls provide room to display Moses's large paintings.

The minimalist approach, the result of a close collaboration between architect and artist, reflects Moses's desire for an un-ostentatious studio and echoes the abstract expressionism of his paintings. Outside, a light scrim provides the artist with an area for painting in the open air.

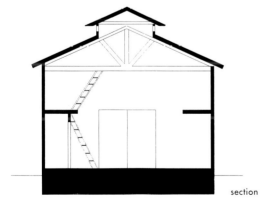

section

20'/6m

I definitely didn't want something conspicuous. I wanted something

I would feel comfortable in. — ED MOSES

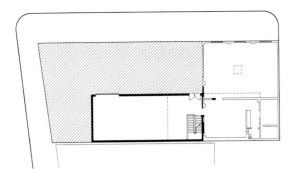

site and first floor plan

Okulick Studio

The minimalist scheme for artist John Okulick's studio incorporates a former gas station, which is transformed into a shop area, and adds a new composing room and gallery. Straightforward and stately, the design reconciles the artist's functional need for abundant, light-filled exhibition and work spaces with his aesthetic requirement for peaceful surroundings.

The 3,600-square-foot studio is both utilitarian and quietly elegant. Outside, the simple rectangular structure is clad in stucco to blend with its industrial surroundings. Inside, the stark white walls rise 28 feet, interrupted by three strategically placed north-facing windows, to provide large wall spaces suitable for creative work and gallery viewing. The 20-foot-wide space is crowned with a bowstring steel truss system and six translucent skylights.

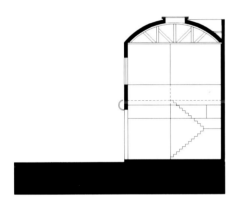

cross section

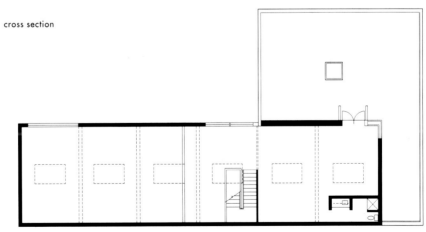

second floor plan

|— — — — —| 20'/6m

This vertical space, awash with light, is like walking into a snowstorm in which John Okulick's sculptures emerge from whiteness. — SE

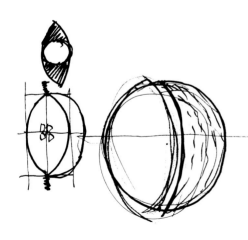

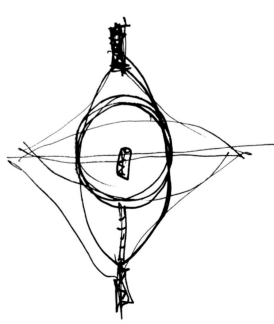

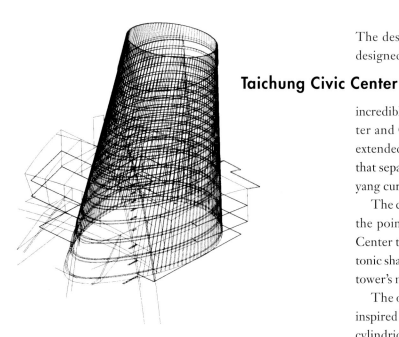

City Council Chambers, computer rendering

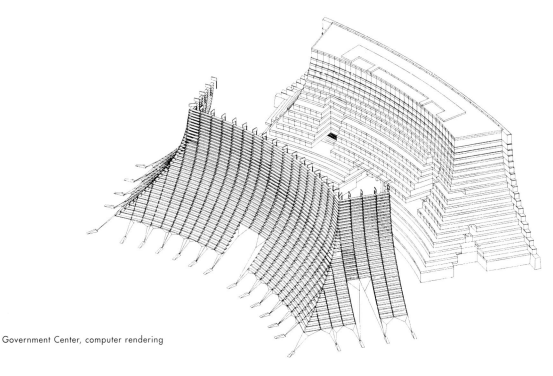

Government Center, computer rendering

Taichung Civic Center

The design of this new 2,000,000-square-foot civic center, designed with HCCH as executive architects, finds its roots in Chinese tradition, but also embraces the complex dualities of a Taiwanese culture changing with incredible speed. Its two major structures, a Government Center and City Council Chambers, face each other across an extended plaza—a site for everyday and festival gatherings—that separates gardens from hardscaping with a sweeping yin-yang curve.

The curved roofline of traditional Chinese temples became the point of departure for the eighteen-story Government Center tower, with its concave face. At the same time, its tectonic shading devices and high-tech tent-like skin proclaim the tower's modernity.

The oval plan of the City Council Chambers building was inspired by the donor lamps found in Buddhist temples—large cylindrical structures that held votive candles (or, today, often electric light bulbs). Linked in their symbolism and evoking deeply held Chinese values, the Government Center and the City Council Chambers are expressive icons for a new Taiwan.

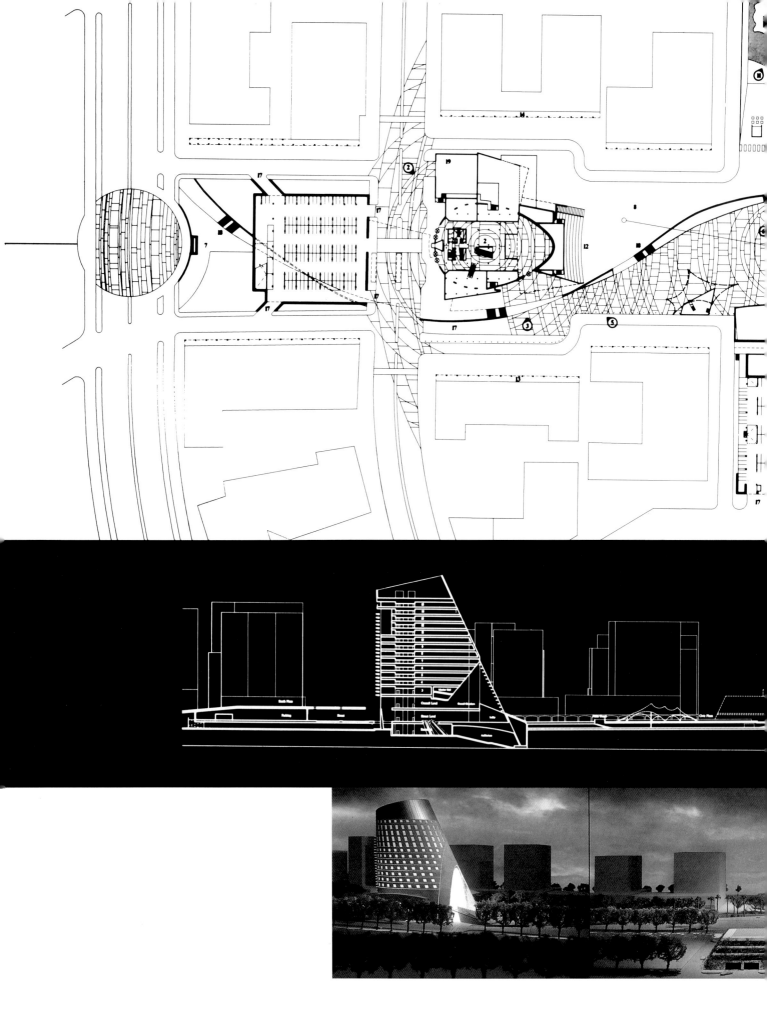

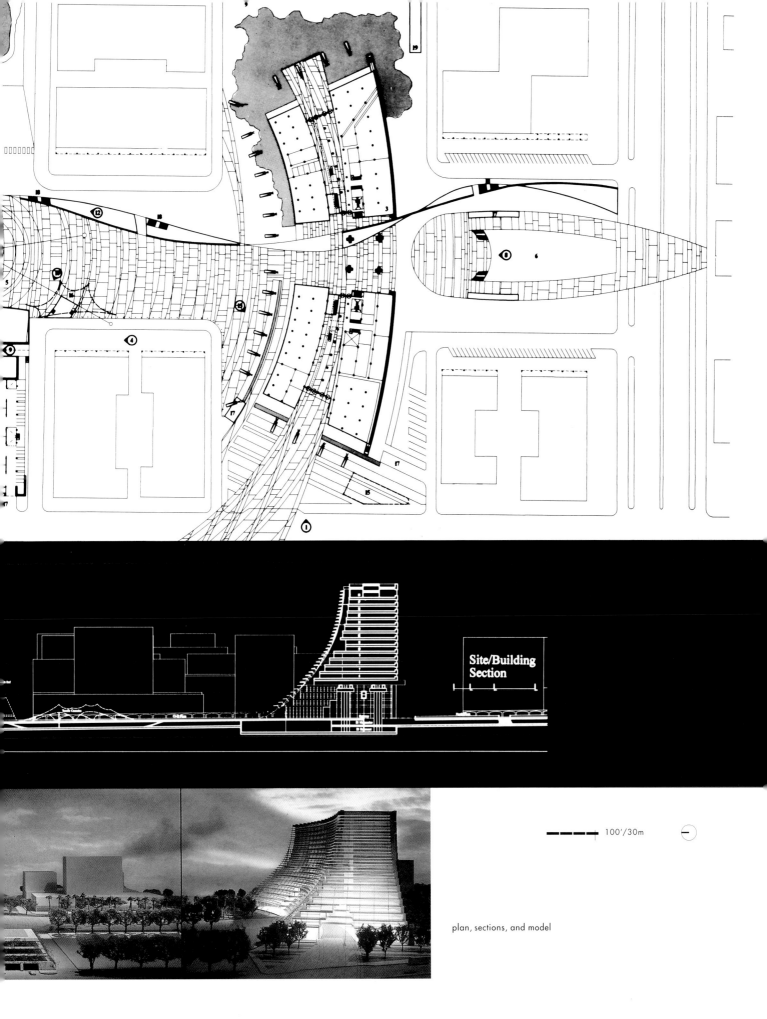

Site/Building
Section

100'/30m

plan, sections, and model

This complex's roots are founded in Chinese history and culture.

Traditional temple roof

The design belongs in Taiwan and interprets vernacular symbols using high technology in a practical way. — SE

Temple donor lamps

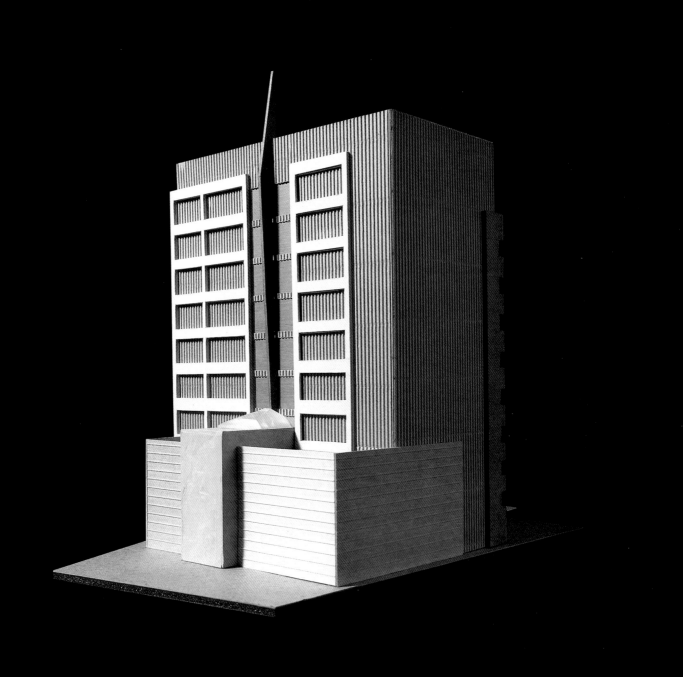

Taipei Tower

This eleven-story tower in downtown Taipei continues the cross-cultural fusion of the Ahmadu Bello University Theater (p. 68), the Futiko-Tamagowon reception center (p. 62), and the Taichung Civic Center (p. 200). The first three stories consist of a shopping center. Local tradition dictates a covered arcade extension at the ground floor level, which penetrates the basal plinth at the street frontage. Above the shopping center level, eight stories of office space are clad in a high-tech skin of stainless steel, glass, and granite.

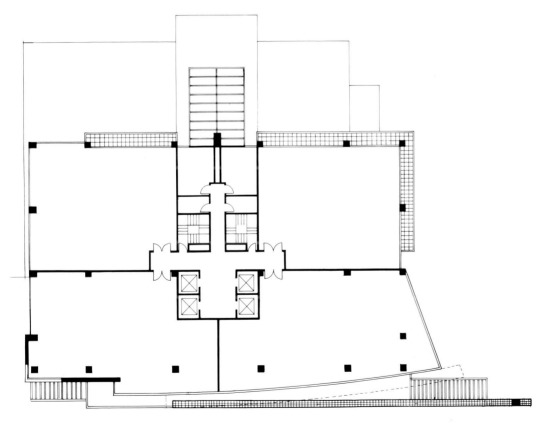

typical office plan

33'/10m

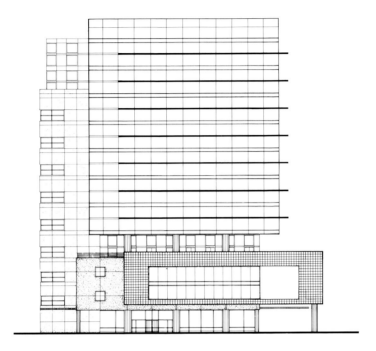

south elevation

This project continues to explore the fusion of Eastern and Western cultures and ideas. Each nourishes the other to find a new hybrid architecture for the Pacific Rim. — NS

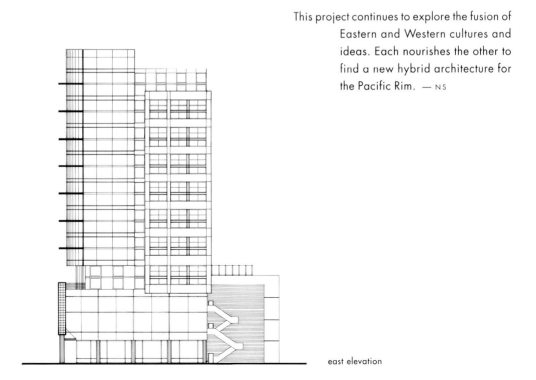

east elevation

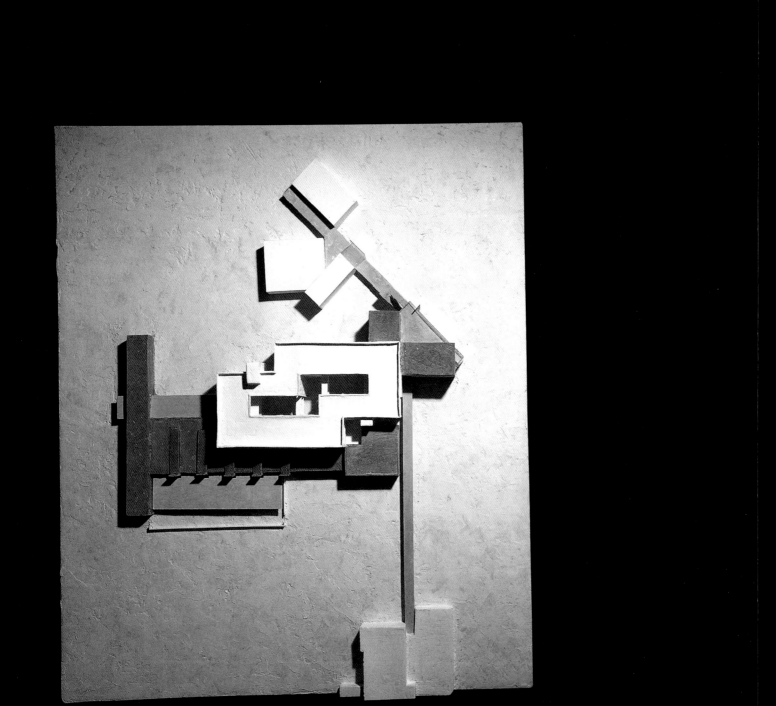

Orange Coast College Art Center

The Art Center, located at the vertex of two green belts, splices into the visual lines of force uniting the college campus. The Center pulls the gaze southward to the articulated facade of its three-story "head." The head is connected to a three-story block of classrooms and studios that will be built of cast-in-place concrete. This piece is bisected through its full height by a clerestory-lit space, which connects all three stories visually and provides amply lit walls for student art.

The third and final element completing the composition is the one-story steel industrial portion. This houses the ground-floor heavier industrial uses, such as sculpture and ceramics. It is characterized by north-facing light monitors that rhythmically bring light into the inner studio spaces of the Art Center.

site plan

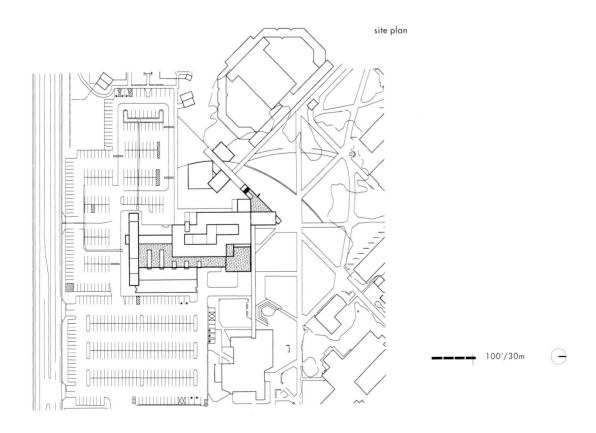

100'/30m

20'/6m

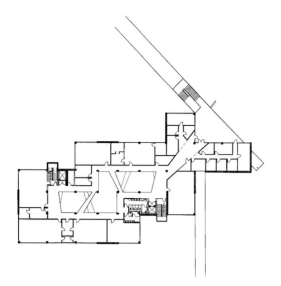

third floor plan

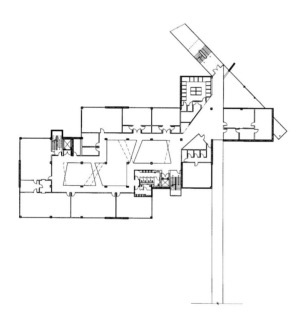

second floor plan

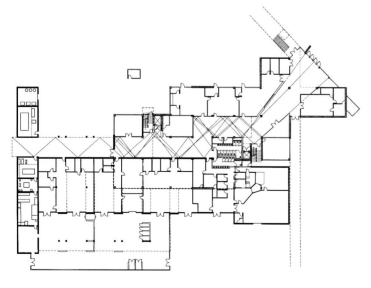

first floor plan

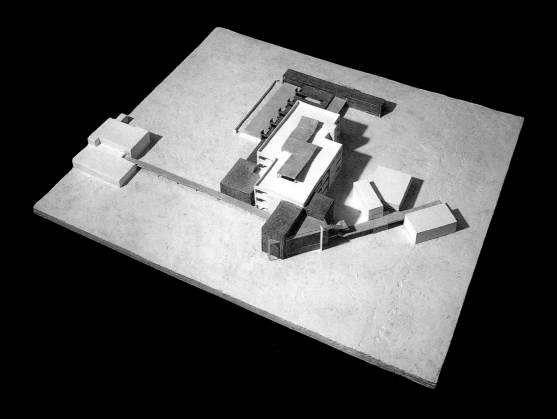

The Art Center's "head" acts not only as a magnet, drawing people toward it, but also as an amplifier announcing, in visual terms, the importance of the arts. — SE

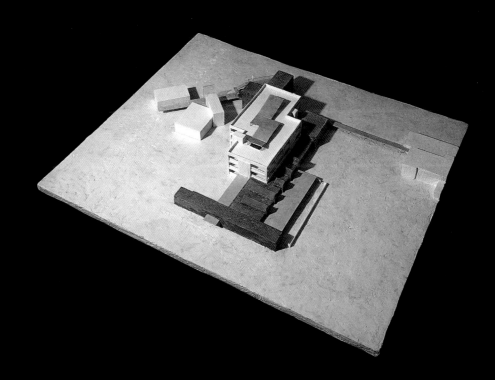

From Djene to the Chinese-Paris Border: An Architectural Journey

Steven Ehrlich

My arrival by dugout canoe in 1975 at the ancient city of Djene, in the West African country of Mali, culminated an architectural pilgrimage begun in 1969 in Morocco. Djene—near Timbuctou and long an Islamic commercial center on the upper Niger River—is home to the Djene Mosque, the world's largest mud structure, which I had come to experience. Massive and primal, built from the soil upon which it stands, the mosque exudes a powerful organic simplicity. It was a spirit I had encountered in Morocco, Nigeria, and other countries in and around the Sahara desert during a six-year post-university African sojourn during which I practiced, taught, and observed architecture. As I traveled, I admired the clarity of purpose embodied in this "architecture without architects." From West Africa's large mud mosques to the everyday vernacular of round thatched huts and earthen granaries scattered across the savanna, these buildings shared an economy of means and a direct connection to the materials and climate of their surroundings. They were the expression of cultures deeply and harmoniously rooted in their environment. This understanding, absorbed as I sketched and photographed at the beginning of my career, etched a deep impression in my thinking about architecture.

1

2

More than twenty years later in Los Angeles, the Robertson Branch Library (1993–97) reflects the enduring imprint of West Africa and the Djene Mosque on my work. The structure, located on a busy thoroughfare, must vie for attention with a strip mix of traffic, billboards, and commercial buildings. Its preweathered, copper-clad "ship's hull" protrudes over the sidewalk and breaks the building's rectangular street elevation with a simple yet sculpturally energetic form, announcing its presence on the street and declaring its cultural purpose as a vessel of society's learning.

The period between my encounter with the Djene Mosque and the design for the Robertson Branch Library comprises an ongoing journey of exploration, a gradual yet constant evolution and refining of my ideas about urban architecture and the relationship of structures to the surrounding city and the natural environment.

My travels in Africa, Latin America, and Asia have instilled in me a sensitivity to cultural traditions, which I term "architectural anthropology." I quickly learned to admire the quiet of interior courtyards, the straightforward organic response of indigenous housing, and the tranquillity of Buddhist shrines. At the same time, I have delighted in cross-tribal encounters and the bustling excitement of African and Asian marketplaces.

This philosophy of architectural anthropology permeates my approach to modernism. In embracing both, I adhere to the premise that simplicity and clarity are the best guides. Even as my designs become more complex, I proceed from straightforward architectural concepts. In my residential projects, especially, I seek to achieve a serenity that balances tranquillity and repose with a visceral impact that connects us to nature. At the same time, I seek to infuse public buildings, with their more complex purposes and more diverse

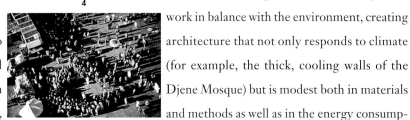

4

5

populations, with the spontaneous social energy and cultural fusion of non-Western market-places.

Today my approach to design continues to evolve, not only as a result of continuing travel and reflection, but through close collaboration with my partner in Steven Ehrlich Architects, Nick Seierup, and all the other talented architects in our firm. Nick has traveled and studied widely in Asia, and he and I share an appreciation of the vernacular and a sensitivity to cultural traditions. Together we practice a creative fusion of modernism and architectural anthropology.

Modernism and
Vernacular—Complement and Counterpoint

I received my architectural training at a time when the International Style was at its zenith, particularly in American urban architecture, and I maintain a steady faith in Louis Sullivan's adage that "form follows function." Still, I don't view this credo as an unbending intellectual ideology. Buildings exist, after all, to serve people. They need to embody the dreams and gregariousness of human life. They must resolve issues, and make living, working, and cultural pursuits more enjoyable for the people who use them. Function remains fundamental, while form and space are more flexible, lending themselves to an intuitive approach to the symbolic and emotional components of a design.

Our architecture strives for modernity in-

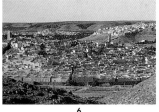

6

7

8

formed by the simplicity and directness of vernacular forms. Indigenous builders everywhere work in balance with the environment, creating architecture that not only responds to climate (for example, the thick, cooling walls of the Djene Mosque) but is modest both in materials and methods as well as in the energy consumption required to build and support it. The native builders in nonindustrial cultures never strayed from the precept, championed by Frank Lloyd Wright in his "organic architecture," that architecture is a responsive servant of nature.

The environmentalists of today's "green architecture" movement, rediscovering that vision, have begun again to listen to the land and look to the vernacular. As the advocates of "critical regionalism" point out, the indigenous built environment, whether it consists of thick-walled adobes or stone-walled courtyard complexes, represents an efficient response to a local environment, evolved over decades and centuries. This lesson becomes a powerful tool in the hands of those with a modernist bent. It reminds us that materials and design should be the basis for livability, not the application of technological "muscle" in an attempt to overcome the environment.

The Schulman house (1989–92), a large residence tucked into a Southern California canyon, embodies this syncretism of site and sensibility. Before the first sketches, before the first computer keystrokes, I listened both to the landscape and to the owners' desires and dreams for their home. That listening led to the logic for the design. To conform to the curve of the surrounding canyon wall, I skewed the H-shaped parti by angling one wing of the house. This adaptation not only respects the contours of the site, but dramatically energizes the initially symmetrical order of the plan. The welcoming forecourt was designed to preserve a mature sycamore tree, maintaining a link to the native flora. To make this possible, garages were buried, out of sight, into the canyon wall.

The marriage of the modern and the vernacular is not restricted to new construction, however. Adaptive modification of old buildings provides the chance to preserve vernacular roots, while "turbocharging" structures for new functions.

9

BUS Wellness Center (1995–96) offers a good example. The owners wished to convert an unused Greyhound bus terminal in downtown Santa Monica to a health club and wellness center. By performing some "architectural archeology," Nick was able to peel away the accretions of previous remodelings to discover a beautiful 1950s steel, tapered girder roof frame, now dis-

10

creetly revealed to the street in the redesign. The owner accepted my suggestion to name the new establishment BUS as a way of retaining the building's original sign on the street. This decision not only saved the eponymous reminder of the site's former use, but preserved a historical (by Los Angeles's standards, at least) artifact in Santa Monica, where Greyhound has gone the way of the twenty-five-cent milkshake. In many cases, re-storing historical form with a reinvented func-

11

tion in this manner provides a viable and eco-nomical means to renew American cities while preserving architectural tradition.

Los Angeles—
The Incubator of Change

The importance of this syncretic blend of vernacular and modern is equalled by the influence of Los Angeles—its unusually benign climate, which favors patios and open windows, and the rich multicultural environment provided by its many ethnic groups. The city possesses, moreover, a rich heritage of California regional design in the work of such architects as Julia Morgan, Greene and Greene, and Irving Gill. Pioneering modernist architects such as Rudolph Schindler, Richard Neutra, and Ray Kappe found here a fertile field for their work. And Los Angeles is home to boldly original works by Frank Lloyd Wright, John Lautner, and Frank Gehry.

Viewed from an airplane, the grid of Los Angeles's streets and freeways stretches like a giant computer chip to the horizon. The resemblance is not only figurative. Los Angeles is a computer-age center oriented toward the future, and its grid embodies a city on the move, a vast network packet-switching people from home to work or business to business. It symbolizes the city's nearly limitless ability to respond instantly to new information and reconfigure itself to constant change.

It was this sense of potentiality that drew me to Los Angeles following my African sojourn. The city pulses with the economic energy of a great metropolis of the Pacific Century. In addition, with its immigrant colonies from Latin America and Asia, it is bursting with the social energy sparked wherever multiple cultures converge. From reggae sushi bars to its strip of Ethiopian restaurants near the heart of the heavily Jewish Fairfax district, this city dances to a world beat.

I find curiously attractive the seeming monotony of Los Angeles's largely nondescript streetscape—the energetic visual clutter of signs and billboards along the miles-long boulevards lined with one- and two-story shops, houses, and mini-malls, and the sprawling colonias in the San Fernando Valley and the Westside comprised of what Rayner Banham called "dingbat" apartment buildings, and, closer to downtown, the older brick walk-ups crowded with the city's recently arrived residents.

In my work, I respond emotionally to all these facets of Los Angeles. The Shatto Recreation Center (1987–90), for example, represents a strongly intuitive response to the challenge of designing a building tough enough for an inner-city neighborhood, yet still inviting to streetwise kids of different ethnic groups.

Early in the design process, I felt that the solution must lie in a building, like the Djene Mosque, that stated its presence simply, yet powerfully. The central concept—the curve of Shatto's bold, sweeping roofline—came to me at the beach. The curling breakers inspired the idea for a wavelike curve, dynamically accelerating and decelerating. The curve would fit easily with the Center's utilitarian rectangular footprint, yet stand out gracefully, softening the surrounding cityscape.

Shatto's curving back gave rise to a "whale" metaphor, which I playfully elaborated with a finlike sunshade over the entry. (The center was soon fondly nicknamed "The Whale" by local residents.) The abstract, calligraphic patterns of the structural masonry walls were designed in collaboration

12

13

14

15

16

with artist Ed Moses and further proclaim the artistic impulse at the root of this building. The art evokes Los Angeles's well known tradition of wall murals and taps into a current of demotic art appreciation: the building has remained "untagged" by graffiti (perhaps because the "graffiti" are built in).

The roofline of the Child Care Center (1992–95) presents a more complex accelerating and decelerating glissando of curves than Shatto's, with the street front and rear elevations offering vertical mirror images of each other. Inside, the complex undulation of the exposed roof gives an expansive spaciousness in some areas and cozy snugness in others. Yet, despite its drama, the roof covers a simple, versatile parti. With the Child Care Center, as with Shatto, intuition lies at the root of the design, making the structure joyous and playful, in keeping with its function.

Courtyards—Looking Inward

If the progression in my work as I have outlined so far represents an evolving, increasingly complex design response to the relationship between modern and vernacular forms, Los Angeles's urban environment, and more complex commissions, the origins of another theme—the urban courtyard—go back to a much earlier stage in my journey when I went to Morocco in 1969 as a U.S. Peace Corps volunteer. For the next two years I lived in the ancient city of Marrakech, working as the first Peace Corps architect in the Moroccan Ministry of Urban Development and

Housing at about the time Crosby, Stills, and Nash's song "Marrakech Express" topped the music charts.

Morocco, with cities dating from the Middle Ages, has long contended with the issues of densely concentrated urban life. In fact, the population density of Marrakech rivals that of Manhattan. Yet, unlike Manhattan, you notice immediately when you fly over Marrakech that each house possesses an interior courtyard—a cool oasis perfumed with orange blossoms and enlivened by the spill of water in tiled fountains.

17

Over the centuries, Moroccans have refined the urban residential courtyard as a "green" solution to North Africa's fierce sun and to the challenge of finding quietude in crowded cities. There is a deeper meaning to the Moroccan courtyard as well: Islamic tradition holds that each man's private space must be cultivated to resemble Paradise. The courtyard represents a symbolic Garden of Eden, linking residents to God and nature.

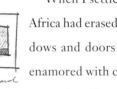

18

I realized I had found an architectural antidote to what I call "the crust of civilization"—the rapid growth of urbanism with its sensory overload and information glut. In the United States, particularly, houses occupy an ever greater portion of lots that for economic reasons are growing smaller, and homeowners find their vistas shrinking—or worse yet, filled with the neighbor's wall. Courtyards solve this problem by focusing inward.

19

In later travels, I observed that the Japanese, who have contended with urban living for at least a thousand years longer than we have in the U.S., have also evolved an inward focus in their architecture. *Ryokans*, or traditional Japanese inns, possess an entry court-

yard where the freshness of shrubs and the murmur of fountains disengage the visitor from the noise of street and city. Houses and apartments have a *tokonoma*, an altar-like niche for flower arrangements or a bonsai tree. Meditation centered on the bonsai can remove the Japanese city dweller, as if by astral projection, to a forest far removed from Tokyo or Osaka.

When I settled in Los Angeles, my years in Africa had erased my East Coast notions of windows and doors as barriers to weather. I was enamored with courtyard architecture and climates that allowed one to savor the outdoors all year long.

Los Angeles has proved a fine location to explore courtyard designs. Angelenos celebrate the sun and revel in beaches and gardens. Patio and pool serve as outdoor living rooms. Southern California's climate encourages us to find ways to dissolve the boundaries between interior and exterior. This, in turn, requires us to analyze more closely the dialogue between structures and their settings, since the courtyard places the outdoors "inside" the house. Moreover, new and constantly emerging technologies and materials—glass, metals, sealants, and the mechanisms to control them—multiply the ways to decompose the barrier between indoors and out.

The Farrell house (1993–95) illustrates how the courtyard "edits out" the crust of civilization, while connecting people directly to a focused, natural setting. The owner, a rock musician who spends a great deal of time on the road, wanted a home that

20

would provide at once a haven and easy access to an outdoor lap pool. The two-story barrel-vault "basilica" at the center of the design includes a glass wall

21

facing the pool, which slides completely away into a wall pocket, erasing the indoor-outdoor barrier. A "get wet" linoleum living room floor and "bleacher seating" steps form an easy transition between the living room and the swimming pool.

In the case of an addition to a beach house by Richard Neutra, the courtyard concept provided the organizing principle for integrating an existing house, designed by Neutra in 1938, with the addition of an entertainment pavilion and pool, conceived when the current homeowner acquired the adjacent lot. A new two-story wing, built at a right angle to the long, rectangular Neutra house, creates an L-shaped parti and forms a barrier to the busy Pacific Coast Highway below, blocking traffic noise and the distraction of passing cars. The pavilion, with its silvery stainless steel shell and glass walls, seems to float like a soap bubble in the courtyard created within the L-shaped parti.

If the courtyard serves as a residential antidote to the crust of civilization, the piazza—the courtyard's counterpart on the civic scale—provides a strong organizing principle for multistructure commercial or public projects. It's a concept we first explored in designing the West Coast headquarters of Sony Music Entertainment (1991–93), in Santa Monica, and then elaborated in the DreamWorks SKG Animation Studios (1996–98) in Glendale.

The Animation Studios occupy a 13-acre triangular site next to the Los Angeles River. The five-building complex provides 320,000 square feet of studio space for a creative corps of more than a thousand artists and technicians who produce the increasingly computer-rendered images of today's motion pictures and video.

DreamWorks desired a setting conducive to outdoor and indoor meetings. The five-building "campus" allows for spontaneous and planned encounters by creating spaces that encourage legs and mind to roam freely. This was accomplished by organizing the complex as a hierarchy of open spaces. Given Los Angeles's more than three hundred sunny days per year, the abundance of outdoor plazas that function as "meeting rooms" provides an inspiring open-air annex to the computer-filled offices inside the buildings. The heart of the Animation Studios consists of a large common plaza, or piazza. Each building, in turn, possesses its own courtyard, all of which spill onto the piazza or front onto the manmade river, which traces a vestigial path of the Los Angeles River. This planning strategy echoes historical European city plans and represents that fertile territory where cultures intersect. The exploration of this virtual territory comprises the fourth major theme in our work.

The Chinese-Paris Border—Cross-Cultural Fusion

Marshall McLuhan foresaw in the 1960s that electronic communications would transform the world into a "global village," breaking down barriers erected by distance and cultural distinctions. Today, the global village is coming into being before our eyes as Brazilian villagers chat on cellular phones and Western physicians study acupuncture and Chinese herbal medicine.

For cross-cultural explorers such as Nick and me, this new era of cultural encounter opens exciting territory for practicing critical region-

23

24

22

alism on a global scale—a "global regionalism" that listens to the land, understanding and respecting cultural traditions and ethnic identities while welcoming innovation and the introduction of new building technologies. For me, the Laughing Man, the hero of a tale by the same name in J. D. Salinger's *Nine Short Stories*, can be seen as a fictional embodiment of a global villager. He is a hyperrealistic character who is constantly crossing the "Chinese-Paris border," a fanciful concept reached only through the imagination. The Laughing Man symbolizes the possibilities that spring from unlikely and unanticipated crossings of cultural borders.

25

Which brings me back to Africa and an early work: the theater I designed in 1976 for Ahmadu Bello University in Zaria, Nigeria. Western dramatic performance differs substantially from traditional African ritual and verbal art. I wanted to create a theater and teaching workshop that would bridge the cultural gap by providing a versatile facility suited to indigenous types of performance, classical Western dramas, and intermediate forms not yet born.

The parti, resembling that of a typical northern Nigerian residential compound, consists of a circular central performance area, enclosed by mud walls with four round mud huts and two square entry rooms, called *soros* in the local Hausa language, at the corners. The central performance area and the smaller spaces provided by the four huts permit many staging arrangements—from a standard stage-plus-proscenium to theater-in-the-round. This fusion of flexible function with traditional forms fits the theater department's goal of producing new African drama while providing a milieu that mixes lessons learned from vernacular architecture with innovations that

26

encourage novel theater.

Two decades later I found myself collaborating not with Hausa builders, but with a master of *feng shui*, an ancient Chinese teaching with the aim of balancing forces to ensure harmony with nature and the cosmos. The project this time was a house for a Taiwanese couple settling in southern California. The collaboration for the Lo house (1995–97) involved a careful balancing between the dictates of *feng shui*, which provided a traditional Chinese matrix based on the nine cells of a three-by-three grid as the main underlying design concept, and my parti based on this form. The resulting structure fuses *feng shui* with Western architecture, with detailing and materials further developing the critical reinterpretation and fulfilling the clients' desire to live in a "Chinese" house. The Lo house is located near Los Angeles, but its conceptual coordinates place it directly astride the Chinese-Paris border.

Latin American culture is the source of cultural fusion in a civic project in San Jose, California. The development occupies nearly a city block and integrates the San Jose redevelopment agency's Biblioteca Latinoamericana (1996–99), a library specializing in Latin American reference works and literature, and a youth center with gym and recreation areas.

The complex—whose large shaded courtyard provides a placita, or mini-plaza, for community fiestas—is a harbinger of the city's revitalization of this largely Latino area near downtown. Fronting on First Street, a major arterial, the development presents a monumental wall, massive yet penetrated by openings and reminiscent of long, low structures found at Mexican archaeological sites such as Teotihuacán and Monte Alban. The face of this monumental

27

wall presents a recurring historic Latin American design motif, engulfed by modern, abstract patterns, all in structural masonry; the resulting palimpsest subtly interweaves references to San Jose's Latin American heritage and its unfolding future. The wall, like the walls of the Shatto Recreation Center, proclaims its origins in art and history. The complex as a whole, designed for a wide range of multicultural community uses, traces its inspiration to the Chinese-Paris border.

Many Borders to Cross

28

The world has changed dramatically since my 1975 pilgrimage to Djene. Advanced telecommunications, the Internet, and nearly universal air transportation have shrunk the globe by accelerating the movement of people, images, and ideas. What we seek to capture in our architectural anthropology, however, has not altered. We attempt to embody in our work the emotional power of the Djene Mosque, with design that flows from the heart as well as the mind. We try to infuse each project with the primacy of place and to accommodate climate and culture, taking advantage of breeze and shade and treading lightly on the land. This approach respects the uniqueness of client and locality and recognizes our responsibility to a planet with limited resources.

29

30

We start by heeding the heartbeat of the land, seeking to sense its character so intimately that the design becomes, in the words of my mathematician friend and client, Howard Swann, a "discovery of the inevitable." This logic of location and the unique goals of each client mean necessarily that a house in Minneapolis will differ from one in Miami, that a civic complex in Taiwan should not be interchangeable with one designed for Toronto. Much of our work, therefore, reflects Los Angeles's kinetic energy.

Appreciation of the vernacular and an intuitive approach to design, combined with the rigor of a rational search for the modern, are the constants in our work. But my personal architectural journey has coincided with the whirlwind globalization of commerce and communications that took off in the 1980s and 1990s, and our clients confront broadening possibilities and increasing complexities. How best to reconcile the constants in our work with the quest for innovative designs for the future?

The answer, I believe, is to recognize the fertility of the cross-cultural fusion at the Chinese-Paris border while minding well the teachings of the vernacular. Failure to do so is to encourage a homogenization of the world's cultures or an architecture of mere pastiche. Globalization represents a chance to fuse into a new paradigm the lessons of indigenous architecture while deepening our appreciation of what is common across cultures. Sensitivity and respect are the keys: it is easy to photograph or sketch a mosque, a villa, or a pagoda, but understanding it only comes from understanding its cultural roots. Any "translation" into modern design must remain faithful to the semiotics of locale. Globalization, understood in this sense, enriches architecture and celebrates its primal purpose of connecting people in a place of beauty and in repose with nature. The belief in this larger purpose guides our continuing journey.

Santa Monica, California

20 October 1997

Awards, Honors, and Exhibits

DESIGN AWARDS

American Institute of Architects

National AIA

1998 AIA/National Concrete Masonry Association: Child Care Center, Culver City, California
1997 Paul Cummins Library, Crossroads School, Santa Monica, California (Architecture)
1997 Schulman House, Brentwood, California (Architecture)
1997 Bow Truss Studio, Sony Pictures Entertainment, Culver City, California (Interiors)
1997 AIA/National American Library Association: Paul Cummins Library, Santa Monica, California
1994 AIA/National Concrete Masonry Association: Shatto Recreation Center, Los Angeles, California

California AIA

1998 *Merit Award*, Paul Cummins Library, Crossroads School, Santa Monica, California
1996 *Merit Award*, Child Care Center, Culver City, California
1995 *Honor Award*, Farrell House, Venice, California
1995 *Merit Award*, Schulman House, Brentwood, California
1991 *Honor Award*, Israel House, Santa Monica, California
1990 *Merit Award*, Windward Circle Redevelopment, Venice, California
1987 *Commendation*, Moses Studio, Venice, California
1984 *Honor Award*, Ahmadu Bello University Theater, Zaria, Nigeria
1982 *Honor Award*, Kalfus Studio, Los Angeles, California

Los Angeles AIA

1997 *Merit Award*, Paul Cummins Library, Crossroads School, Santa Monica, California
1997 *Merit Award*, Child Care Center, Culver City, California
1996 *Merit Award*, BUS Wellness Center, Santa Monica, California
1996 *Merit Award*, Bow Truss Studio, Sony Pictures Entertainment, Culver City, California (Interiors)
1992 *Honor Award*, Schulman House, Los Angeles, California
1992 *Honor Award*, Shatto Recreation Center, Los Angeles, California
1989 *Honor Award*, Okulick Studio, Venice, California
1988 *Merit Award*, Moses Studio, Venice, California
1983 *Honor Award*, Swann House, Santa Cruz, California
1982 *Citation*, Ahmadu Bello University Theater, Zaria, Nigeria
1981 *Honor Award*, Kalfus Studio, Los Angeles, California

INTERNATIONAL AWARDS

1995 *Honorable Mention*, Taichung Civic Center Competition, Taichung, Taiwan

NATIONAL AWARDS

1996 *Architectural Record*, "Record Interiors," BUS Wellness Center, Santa Monica, California
1996 *Merit Award*, Custom Home Award, Farrell House, Venice, California
1995 *Grand Award*, Builder's Choice Award, Hempstead House, Venice, California
1994 *Merit Award*, Builder's Choice Award, Sony Music Entertainment West Coast Headquarters, Santa Monica, Calif.
1992 *Socially Conscious Award*, Interiors Award, Shatto Recreation Center, Los Angeles, California
1990 *Merit Award*, Builder's Choice Award, Miller House, Los Angeles, California
1986 *Merit Award*, Builder's Choice Award, Robertson House, Santa Monica, California

1985 *Grand Award*, Builder's Choice Award, Kalfus Studio, Los Angeles, California
1983 *Honorable Mention*, Builder's Choice Award, Swann House, Santa Cruz, California

REGIONAL AWARDS

1997 *Citation for Unbuilt Projects*, San Diego AIA, Grand Central Arts Building, Santa Ana, California
1997 *Merit Award*, Sunset/AIA Western Home Awards, Farrell House, Venice, California
1996 *Grand Award*, Gold Nugget Award, Bow Truss Studio, Sony Pictures Entertainment, Culver City, California
1995 *Merit Award*, Sunset/AIA Western Home Award, Schulman House, Brentwood, California
1993 *Project of the Year*, Gold Nugget Award, Sony Music Entertainment West Coast Headquarters, Santa Monica, California
1992 *Grand Award*, Concrete Masonry Award, Shatto Recreation Center, Los Angeles, California
1992 *Interior Design Award*, Sunset/AIA Award, Gold-Friedman House, Santa Monica, California
1990 *Merit Award*, Western Red Cedar Lumber Association Design Awards, Moses Studio, Venice, California
1988 *Elan Award*, 268 Townhouses, Chatsworth, California
       Project of the Year, Kaufman and Broad, Pomona, California
1983 *Merit Award*, Sunset/AIA Award, Kalfus Studio, Los Angeles, California

LOCAL AWARDS

1998 Los Angeles Business Council, Robertson Branch Library, Los Angeles, California
1997 Los Angeles Cultural Affairs Commission, Robertson Branch Library, Los Angeles, California
1997 Los Angeles Business Council, Paul Cummins Library, Crossroads School, Santa Monica, California
1997 Los Angeles Business Council, Bow Truss Studio, Sony Pictures Entertainment, Culver City, California
1997 Los Angeles Business Council, BUS Wellness Center, Santa Monica, California
1996 Los Angeles Business Council, Child Care Center, Culver City, California
1996 Los Angeles Business Council, Farrell House, Venice, California
1995 Los Angeles Business Council, Hempstead House, Venice, California
1994 Los Angeles Business Council, Sony Music Entertainment West Coast Headquarters, Santa Monica, California
1994 Los Angeles Business Council, Shatto Recreation Center, Los Angeles, California
1994 Los Angeles Business Council, Schulman House, Los Angeles, California
1994 Los Angeles Business Council, Aspect Ratio, Los Angeles, California
1989 Los Angeles Business Council, Ehrlich House, Santa Monica, California
1989 Los Angeles Cultural Affairs Commission, Shatto Recreation Center, Los Angeles, California

HONORS

1998 City of Los Angeles Resolution of Meritorious Achievement
1997–98 AIA Design Awards Juror: National, New York, Denver, Raleigh-Durham, Los Angeles, San Diego
1997 *Metropolitan Home*, "Design 100 Hall of Fame," March/April
1995 *Architectural Digest*, "The AD 100 Architects & Designers"
1994 *Metropolitan Home*, "Architects We Would Hire"
1993 Fellow of the American Institute of Architects
1989 *Los Angeles Times*, "89 for 1989: The Rising Stars to Watch"

EXHIBITS

1998 "A Contradictory Balance," University of Southern California

1998 "101 New Blood," West Week, Pacific Design Center
(Nick Seierup)

1997 "Steven Ehrlich Architects—World Beat Architecture,"
Hollyhock House, Los Angeles, California

1997 National AIA Award Winners, AIA Convention, New Orleans,
Louisiana (Paul Cummins Library, Bow Truss Studio, Schulman
Residence)

1997 National Library Association Award Winners, San Francisco,
California (Paul Cummins Library)

1997 "Unbuilt Projects" (Tai Chung Civic Center), Boston Society of
Architects, Boston, Massachusetts

1994 Concrete Masonry Award of Excellence Exhibition (Shatto
Recreation Center), AIA National Convention, Los Angeles,
California

1994 "100 Projects 100 Firms 100 Years" (Child Care Center), AIA
National Convention, Los Angeles, California

1994 "Architecture: East/West Exhibition" (Futiko-Tamagowon
Reception Center), Japanese-American National Museum, Los
Angeles, California

1994 "Steven Ehrlich Architect," Hennessey & Ingalls, Santa Monica,
California

1992 "10 California Architects," Royal Institute of British Architects,
London, England

1990 "The Architecture of Steven Ehrlich," Orange Coast College,
Costa Mesa, California

1989 "Pride in Public Architecture Exhibit" (Shatto Recreation
Center), Los Angeles City Hall/Pacific Design Center, Los
Angeles, California

1985 "Tihama Expedition Exhibit," Royal Geographic Society,
London, England

1985 "Interarch 85," Third World Biennial of Architecture, Bulgaria

1985 Ahmadu Bello University Theatre, Nigeria

1984 "1984 Olympic Architects," Museum of Science & Industry, Los
Angeles, California

1983 "Sunset/AIA Award Winners" (Kalfus Studio), AIA Convention,
San Diego, California

1982 "Architecture du Terre" (Ahmadu Bello University Theater),
Centre Pompidou, Paris, France

Selected Bibliography

Steven Ehrlich Architects

Riera Ojeda, Oscar. *Steven Ehrlich Architects: Casas*, CP 67. Madrid:
Kliczkowski, 1998.

"Design Notebook," *New York Times*, 18 June 1998.

"Inside-out," *Detour*, February 1998.

Jodido, Philip. *Contemporary American Architects, Vol. IV*. Cologne:
Taschen, 1998.

Jodido, Philip. *Contemporary American Architects, Vol. III*. Cologne:
Taschen, 1997.

"Urban Vistas," *Rensselaer Magazine*, December 1997.

"Einfacheit und Reduktion, Steven Ehrlich, Santa Monica," *DBZ*,
November 1996.

Jodido, Philip. *Contemporary California Architects*. Cologne: Taschen, 1995.

Nesmith, Eleanor Lynn. *Contemporary World Architects*. Rockport,
Mass.: Rockport, 1994.

"Singergia e Arquitectura: Tres Obras de Steven Ehrlich," *Projecto*,
December 1993.

"An Architect Who Lifts the City's Spirit," *Buzz*, June/July 1993.

"Architects as Artisans," *Design Journal*, December 1991.

"Los Angeles: Une Ville Sous Influence," *City*, November 1990.

"The Tranquil Architecture of Steven Ehrlich," *Interiors & Sources*,
March 1990.

"Studies of the Tihama," *Bulletin of the British Society for Middle East
Studies, Vol. 16*, 1990.

"Deft in Venice," *Angeles Magazine*, March 1989.

"Visual Enrichment," *Connoisseur Magazine*, September 1987.

"Steven D. Ehrlich: Architect," *Our House 8606*, June 1986.

2311 Ocean Front Walk

Stuchin, Marjorie, and Susan Abramson. *Waterside Homes*. Glen Cove,
New York: PBC International, 1998.

"Set Sinks Side by Side," *House Beautiful Kitchens/Baths*, Spring 1997.

Addition to Neutra Beach House

"Steven Ehrlich," *GA Houses 56*, 1998.

"Addition to Neutra Beach House," *Architectural Record*, August 1998.

Zevon, Susan. *Outside Architecture*. Gloucester, Mass.: Rockport, 1998.

Ahmadu Bello University Theater

"ABU Theater Workshop," *Architecture California*, November 1984.

"Mud Theater," *Architectural Design*, December 1976.

BBZ Film Studio

"BBZ Film Ltd.," *Our House 8507*, July 1985.

"Interiors by Architects," *L.A. Architect*, March 1983.

Benenson House

"Steven Ehrlich: Benenson Residence," *GA Houses 55*, May 1998.

Biblioteca Latinoamericana and Washington Area Youth Center

"For Busy Neighborhood, it's 'Bienvenido, Biblioteca'," *San Jose
Mercury News*, 22 March 1998.

"New Bilingual Library and Recreational Center for San Jose,"
Architectural Record, June 1997.

Bow Truss Studio

"1997 Honors and Awards," *Architectural Record*, May 1997.

Jodido, Philip. *Contemporary American Architects, Vol. III*. Cologne:
Taschen, 1997.

"1996 AIA/LA Interior Architecture and Design Awards," *L.A. Architect*,
September 1996.

"Tecnologia turbocopressa, Bow Truss Studio in Culver City," *L'Arca*,
April 1995.

"Games Architects Play," *Architectural Record*, February 1995.

Broadway Deli

"Broadway Deli," *World Space Design*, March 1991.

"Light and Lean," *Restaurant and Hotel Design*, October 1990.

"Great Spaces—The Architects of Dining in L.A.," *Los Angeles Times*, 3 June 1990.

"New Restaurants," *Metropolitan Home*, July 1990.

"L.A. en Parle," *Vogue*, October 1990.

BUS Wellness Center

"The BUS Wellness Center," *L'Arca*, June 1997.

"Public Spaces and Other Projects," *Interiors*, February 1997.

"The Feng Shui Way," *Living Fit*, October 1997.

"From Bus Station to Fitness Center," *Architectural Record*, September 1996.

Child Care Center

Jodido, Philip. *Contemporary American Architects, Vol. III*. Cologne: Taschen, 1997.

"Child Care Center in Culver City," *Space Design*, January 1997.

"La geometrica dello spirito," *L'Arca*, April 1996.

"A Home Away From Home," *Metropolis*, October 1995.

"Kidspace," *Los Angeles Times*, July 9, 1995.

"Specifically Green: 2 New Sustainable Buildings," *L.A. Architect*, April 1995.

"Up and Coming," *Architecture*, February 1993.

Doughty-Vining House

"Vining Residence," *World Residential Design, Vol. I*, March 1990.

"Emotional Architecture: The New Language of Home," *Metropolitan Home*, July 1987.

Douroux House

"Steven Ehrlich: Douroux & Guc Residence," *GA Houses 49*, July 1996.

DreamWorks SKG Animation Studios

"Dream Factory," *Buildings*, August 1997.

"On the Boards," *Architecture*, November 1996.

"DreamWorks SKG Animation Studios" *Theatre Crafts International*, October 1996.

"Hollywood's Fresh Blueprint," *Los Angeles Times Calendar*, 22 September 1996.

"What, Just One Campanile?", *Interiors*, September 1996.

"Themed Architecture and Playa Vista Development," *L.A. Architect*, September 1996.

"Fairy Tale Campus in Glendale to House DreamWorks Animators," *Architectural Record*, August 1996.

Ehrlich House

Zevon, Susan. *Outside Architecture*. Gloucester, Mass.: Rockport, 1998.

"Una Casa A Cuore Aperto," *Brava Casa*, July 1997.

"Easy Living Emphasized," *House Beautiful Kitchens/Baths*, Fall 1997.

"Bring in the Outdoors," *House Beautiful Kitchen/Baths*, Spring 1997.

"Floral Trends, '95," *Flowers & Trends*, January 1995.

"White Light," *Bagno Eaccessori*, May 1991.

"Rigorous Linearity," *L'Ambiente Cucina*, May/June 1991.

"Architect in Residence," *Angeles Magazine*, June 1989.

"Visual Oasis in Urban L.A.," *Los Angeles Times*, 2 April 1989.

Ehrman-Coombs House

Stuchin, Marcie, and Susan Abrahmson. *Waterside Homes*. Glen Cove, New York: PBC International, 1998.

Stuchin, Marcie, and Susan Abrahmson. *Bedrooms and Private Spaces: Designer Dreamscapes*. Glen Cove, New York: PBC International, 1997.

"Slice of Life," *House Beautiful*, May 1996.

Jodido, Philip. *Contemporary California Architects*. Taschen, 1995.

"Narrow Shelves for Kitchen Collectibles," *Sunset*, August 1995.

"Shore Thing," *Architectural Review*, July 1994.

"Guardando l'orizzonte," *Ville Giardini*, May 1994.

"Steven Ehrlich: Israel Residence," *GA Houses 39*, 1993.

"AM Strand," *Moebel Interior Design*, July 1993.

"A Passion for the Pacific," *Self*, July 1993.

"Casa a Los Angeles: Steven Ehrlich," *Abitare Milan*, May 1992.

"Ein Neuer Stern Am Strand Von Santa Monica," *Hauser*, May 1992.

"Conexion sin Perdida de Proteccion," *Architectural Houses*, April 1991.

Farrell House

"Aus der Reihe," *DBZ*, June 1997.

"Perfect Pitch," *Custom Home*, September 1996.

"Venice Vibe," *Architectural Digest*, August 1995.

"Steven Ehrlich," *GA Houses 44*, 1994.

Friedman House

"The Element of Surprise," *Southern California Home & Garden*, August 1988.

"Global Architecture," *GA Houses 21*, 1987.

"Buchalter/Friedman Residence in L.A.," *Our House 8701*, January 1987.

"Friedman Residence," *Our House 8612*, December 1986.

Friedman (Rochdale) House

"Perfect Pools," *House Beautiful*, Spring 1997.

"In the Nature, In the City," *Bagno Eaccessori*, May 1992.

"Nascosto e raffinato il 'nido d'aquila creato da Steven Ehrlich su una collina Los Angeles," *Ville & Casalii*, May 1992.

Futiko-Tamagowon

"Meeting of Two Cultures in a Model Home," *Architecture*, June 1987.

"Selling the Pacific Balance," *Designers West*, March 1987.

"Futiko-Tamagowon," *Our House 8611*, November 1986.

"Tokyo Demonstration House," *Our House 8606*, June 1986.

Gold-Friedman House

Zevon, Susan. *Outside Architecture*. Gloucester, Mass.: Rockport, 1998.

"The Booth Is Back," *Sunset*, January 1996.

"No Uphill Battle," *Better Homes & Gardens*, Winter 1994.

"New Color," *Los Angeles Times Magazine*, 5 April 1992.

"Hillside Hollows," *Los Angeles Times Magazine*, 13 September 1992.

"Scultura da Abitare," *Brava Casa*, April 1992.

Hempstead House

Taylor, Julie. *Outdoor Rooms*. Gloucester, Mass.: Rockport, 1998.

"Statements in Black & White," *Home*, April 1998.

"Sun, Sand & Style Two," *Home*, July/August 1997.

Stuchin, Marcie, and Susan Abrahmson. *Bedroom and Private Spaces: Designer Dreamscapes*. Glen Cove, New York: PBC International, 1997.

Viladas, Pilar. *California Beach Houses: Style, Interiors, and Architecture*. San Francisco: Chronicle Books, 1996.

Jodido, Philip. *Contemporary California Architects*. Cologne: Taschen, 1995.

"Builder's Choice Awards," *Builder*, October 1995.

"Sea of Tranquility," *Los Angeles Times Magazine*, 27 March 1994.

"L.A. Color," *Metropolitan Home*, May/June 1994.

"Steven Ehrlich—Hempstead Residence," *GA Houses* 39, 1993.

Hill Aviation/Logistics

"Hill Aviation/Logistics," *Our House* 8507, July 1985.

Kalfus Studio

Schulman, Julius. *L.A. Obscura: The Architectural Photography of Julius Schulman*. Los Angeles: Fisher Gallery, 1995.

"La Villa Sur La Colline," *Maison Francaise*, July 1987.

Street-Porter, Timothy. *Free Style*. New York: Stewart, Tabori & Chang, 1986.

Conran, Terence. *Terence Conran's New House Book*. London: Conran Octopus Limited, 1985.

"Kalfus Studio," *Our House* 8508, August 1985.

"Steven D. Ehrlich—Kalfus Studio/Guest House," *GA Houses* 15, 1985.

"CCAIA Award Winners," *Architecture California*, January 1983.

"Discovery," *AIA Journal*, December 1982.

"The, '80s Carriage House," *Metropolitan Home*, September 1982.

"Steel & Glass," *Domus*, May 1982.

"Studio/House New Trend Setter from California," *New York Times*, 8 April 1982.

"The Virtue of Simplicity," *Los Angeles Times Home Magazine*, 13 December 1981.

Kuhn House

"New Renovations," *Sunset Magazine*, April 1983.

Lo House

"Pacific Overtures," *Metropolitan Home*, May/June 1998.

"Going with the Flow," *Los Angeles Times Magazine*, 3 May 1998.

Miller-Nazarey House

Soucek King, Carol. *Designing with Glass: The Creative Touch*. Glen Cove, New York: PBC International, 1996.

"Giappone Anni, '90," *Casa America*, October 1991.

"Miller Residence by Steven Ehrlich," *World Residential Design*, Vol. 1, 1990.

"Nature," *Designers West*, October 1989.

Moses Studio

"Ed Moses in Venice," *Architectural Digest*, May 1996.

"Simply Stated," *Los Angeles Times Magazine*, 7 February 1988.

"LA/AIA Awards," *L.A. Architect*, November 1987.

"Specifying Art," *Designers West*, April 1987.

Nesburn House

"Breaking the Modern Mold," *Los Angeles Times Magazine*, 20 July 1997.

Taichung Civic Center

"LA/AIA," *L.A. Architect*, November 1995.

"Steven Ehrlich Architects," *Chinese Architect*, August 1995.

Okulick Studio

"Concrete Dreams" *L.A. Style*, July 1989.

Orange Coast College Art Center

"Plum Jobs," *Interiors*, January 1991.

"OCC Hires Architect for $11 Million Art Center," *Los Angeles Times*, 25 August 1990.

"Designer Chosen for OCC's Art Center," *Daily Pilot*, 25 August 1990.

"OCC Arts Center Design Set," *Orange County Register*, 4 June 1990.

Paul Cummins Library

"Winners of the 1997 Award of Excellence," *Computers in Libraries*, September 1997.

"Honors and Awards," *Architectural Record*, May 1997.

"Biblioteca Paul Cummins in Santa Monica, California," *L'Arca*, May 1997.

"Applauding Excellence in Design," *American Libraries*, April 1997.

"Premio a una buena lectura," *El Cronista Arquitectura*, 16 July 1997.

Robertson Branch Library

"Reading and Riding," *Architecture*, May 1998.

"La quilla del conocimento," *El Cronista Arquitectura*, December 1997.

"One for the Books," *Los Angeles Times*, 7 July 1997.

"Not by the Book," *The Outlook*, 17 June 1997.

Robertson House

"New Yard Scenes," *Builder Magazine*, October 1986.

"Abitare in California," *Domus*, December 1985.

"Robertson Residence," *Our House* 8505, May 1985.

"Robertson Residence," *Sunset Magazine*, April 1983.

"Reninventing the Backyard," *Metropolitan Home*, October 1982.

Saddlerock Ranch

"Saddlerock Ranch," *Our House* 8509, September 1985.

Santa Monica College Library, Remodeling and Addition

"On the Boards," *Architecture*, November 1995.

Schulman House

"Inside-out," *Detour Magazine*, February 1998.

"1997 Honors and Awards," *Architectural Record*, May 1997.

"Winners," *Wall Street Journal*, 13 December 1996.

Soucek King, Carol. *Designing with Wood: The Creative Touch*. Glen Cove, New York: PBC International, 1995.

Riera Ojeda, Oscar. *The New American House*. New York: Whitney, 1995.

"19 Award-Winning Homes," *Sunset Magazine*, September 1995.

Vaugn, John, and Pilar Viladas. *Los Angeles: A Certain Style*. San Francisco: Chronicle, 1995.

"La Casa Nel Canyon," *L'Arca*, September 1994.

"Shore Thing," *Architectural Review*, July 1994.

"Sinergia e Arquitectura: Tres Obras de Steven Ehrlich," *Projecto*, December 1993.

"Steven Ehrlich: Canyon Residence," *GA Houses* 39, 1993.

Shatto Recreation Center

Toy, Maggie. *World Cities: Los Angeles*. London: Academy Editions, 1994.

"Sinergia e Arquitectura: Tres Obras de Steven Ehrlich," *Projecto*, December 1993.

"A City Behind Walls," *Newsweek*, 5 October 1992.

"Gym Dandy," *Los Angeles Times Magazine*, 15 March 1992.

"A Belly Full of Play," *Interiors*, January 1992.

"Street Smarts," *Architecture*, September 1991.

Sony Music Entertainment West Coast Headquarters

Toy, Maggie. *World Cities: Los Angeles*. London: Academy Editions, 1994.

"Contro La Noia," *L'Arca*, March 1994.

"Sinergia e Arquitectura: Tres Obras de Steven Ehrlich," *Projecto*, December 1993.

"Steven Ehrlich," *Interior Design*, November 1993.

"Sony Music Entertainment," *Designers West*, February 1993.

"Sony Music Hits High Note," *Design*, December 1992.

Swann House

"Swann House," *Monterey Life*, November 1985.

"Abitare in California," *Domus*, December 1985.

"Magical Ridge in Santa Cruz," *Our House* 8509, September 1985.

"Small Custom Home Wins Design Award," *Builder*, October 1983.

"L.A. AIA Award Winners," *L.A. Architect*, November 1983.

Windward Circle Redevelopment

"The House with the Waterfall," *Bagno Eaccessori*, August 1992.

"CCAIA Award Winners," *Architectural Record*, July 1990.

"Windward Circle," *Southern California Home and Garden*, April 1990.

"Neighborhood-Friendly Designs," *Los Angeles Times*, 29 April 1990.

"A Renaissance in the New Venice," *Los Angeles Times*, 12 April 1990.

"A Venice, Quasi Una Piazza," *Abitare*, April 1990.

"The New Stone Age," *Home*, April 1990.

"Kuhlek Askese," *German Vogue*, January 1990.

"Lively Definition," *Architecture*, December 1989.

"Venice," *L.A. Style*, July 1989.

"Windward Circle Projects," *Interiors*, March 1987.

"Deft in Venice," *Angeles Magazine*, March 1987.

World Savings and Loan (Thousand Oaks)

"World Savings and Loan," *Our House* 8507, July 1985.

"Monterey Design Conference," *Architecture California*, June 1984.

By Steven Ehrlich

"Africa #1," *Our House* 8611, November 1986.

"Africa #2," *Our House* 8612, December 1986.

"Studies on the Tihama." In *Tihama Expedition, Yemen*. London: Longmans Press, 1985.

Buildings and Projects

LIBRARIES

1999 Biblioteca Latinoamericana & Washington Youth Center, RDA San Jose, California (with Garcia-Teague Architects + Interiors)
1997 Robertson Branch Library, Los Angeles, California
1996 Paul Cummins Library, Crossroads School, Santa Monica, California
1995 Santa Monica College Library (Addition and Renovation Project), Santa Monica, California

RECREATION

1998 Cleveland High School Gymnasium, Reseda, California
1990 Shatto Recreation Center, Los Angeles, California

CAMPUSES

1998 DreamWorks SKG Animation Studios, Glendale, California (with Gensler)
1996 Pixar Village (Project), Emeryville, California
1995 Taichung Civic Center (Project), Taichung, Taiwan (with HCCH)
1992 Sony Music Entertainment West Coast Headquarters, Santa Monica, California

ADAPTIVE REUSE

1998 Grand Central Arts building, California State Fullerton, Santa Ana, California (with Robbins Jergen Christopher)
1998 10865 Washington Boulevard, Culver City, California
1996 BUS Wellness Center, Santa Monica, California
1994 Bow Truss Studio, Sony Pictures Entertainment, Culver City, California

SCHOOLS

2000 Orange Coast College Art Center, Costa Mesa, California
1998 135th Street School, Los Angeles Unified School District (Renovation), Los Angeles, California
1998 186th Street School, Los Angeles Unified School District (Renovation), Los Angeles, California
1997 Cleveland High School (Renovation), Reseda, California

1995 Child Care Center, Culver City, California
1976 Ahmadu Bello University Theater, Zaria, Nigeria
1973 Westminster West Elementary School, Westminster West, Vermont

ART: STUDIOS, GALLERIES

1989 Ellison Studio (Interior), Venice, California
1989 Okulick Studio, Venice, California
1987 Moses Studio, Venice, California
1986 Dill Studio, Venice, California
1985 Pence Art Gallery (Interior), Santa Monica, California
1981 Kalfus Studio, Hollywood Hills, California

MIXED USE

1994 Warner Bros. Entertainment City (Study), Burbank, California (with Landmark Entertainment)
1989 Ace Marketplace, Venice, California
1988 Windward Circle Arts Building, Venice, California
1987 Race Through the Clouds, Venice, California
1986 Futiko-Tamagowon Reception Center, Tokyo, Japan (with Yamada & Associates)

OFFICE

1998 Seven Summits (Interior), Los Angeles, California
1998 Ten9Fifty (Renovation), Culver City, California
1997– Tai Pei Tower, Tai Pei, Taiwan
1994 Warner Bros. Tower (Project), Burbank, California
1988 Pogen Family Bakery (Interior), Compton, California
1988 Aspect Ratio (Interior), Hollywood, California
1987 L.A. Unified School District Offices (Renovation), Los Angeles, California
1984 Hill Aviation Logistics (Interior), Chatsworth, California
1983 Indian Medical Clinic (Interior), Los Angeles, California
1980 BBZ Film Studio (Interior), Venice, California
1978 Sunlight Pictures (Interior), Los Angeles, California

RETAIL

1999 Universal Studios Digital Image Capture Venue, Orlando, Florida
1999 World Savings and Loan (Interior), Santa Monica, California
1999 World Savings and Loan, Thousand Oaks, California
1997 World Savings and Loan (Interior), Rancho Bernardo, California
1996 French Connection (Interior), Santa Monica, California
1995 World Savings and Loan (Interior), Laguna Hills, California
1992 Broadway Deli, Encino, California
1992 Daily Grill Restaurant, Los Angeles, California
1990 Broadway Deli, Santa Monica, California
1990 Daily Grill Restaurant, Brentwood, California
1989 World Savings and Loan (Interior), Seal Beach, California
World Savings and Loan (Interior), Thousand Oaks, California
1987 Next Hair Salon (Interior), Santa Monica, California
1982 Main Street Auto Center (Interior), Santa Monica, California

MULTIFAMILY RESIDENTIAL

1991 Villa Del Este Condominiums, Corona del Mar, California
1989 California West Townhouses, Chatsworth, California
1989 Kaufman & Broad (Housing Development), Pomona, California
1985 Sundance Housing Development, Corona, California
1984 Sundance Housing Development, Rialto, California
1972 Housing for New Rural Villages, Marrakech, Morocco

SINGLE FAMILY RESIDENTIAL

2000 Koffler House, Pacific Palisades, California
1999 Lowe House, Los Angeles, California
1999 St. John House, Cayucos, California
1998 Benensen House, Rustic Canyon, Los Angeles, California

1998 Munitz House (Renovation), Santa Monica, California
1998 Woods House (Renovation), Santa Monica, California
1998 Addition to Neutra Beach House, Santa Monica, California
1997 Lo House, Diamond Bar, California
1997 Richards-Ebert House, Telluride, Colorado
1996 Hayashida House, Kobe, Japan
1996 Biya House, Younde, Cameroons
1996 Margolin House (Renovation), Crestwood Hills, California
1995 Matchinger House (Interior), Santa Barbara, California
1995 Farrell House, Venice, California
1994 Fogelson House (Renovation), Santa Monica, California
1994 Norred House, Malibu, California
1993 Abrams House (Renovation), Beverly Hills, California
1993 Merrit-Harrington House (Interior), Redondo Beach, California
1993 B. Israel House (Renovation), Brentwood, California
1993 Hempstead House, Venice, California
1992 D. Israel House (Renovation), Los Angeles, California
1992 Schulman House, Brentwood, California
1991 Douroux House, Venice, California
1991 Gold-Friedman House, Santa Monica, California
1991 Jenson House, Malibu, California
1990 Youngblood House, Pacific Palisades, California
1990 Freidman House, Crestwood Hills, California
1990 Ehrman/Coombs House, Santa Monica, California
1990 Nesburn/Friedman House, Brentwood, California
1990 Chiate House, Malibu, California
1990 Gilbert-Ray House (Renovation), Los Angeles, California
1990 Plattner House, New Scotland, New York
1990 2311 Ocean Front Walk, Venice, California
1989 Ripple House, Venice, California
1988 Ehrlich House, Santa Monica, California
1987 Wellman House (Renovation), Pacific Palisades, California
1987 Hyman House (Renovation), Brentwood, California
1987 Robertson House, Sun Valley, Idaho
1986 Miller-Nazarey House, Los Angeles, California
1985 Kupperberg House (Renovation), Los Angeles, California
1984 Vining-Doughty House, Lambertville, New Jersey
1984 Buchalter-Freidman House, Brentwood, California
1982 Landers House (Renovation), Beverly Hills, California
1982 Semler House, Malibu, California
1982 Damji House (Renovation), Pacific Palisades, California
1981 Robertson House (Renovation), Santa Monica, California
1981 Hogle-Sisk House (Renovation), Los Angeles, California
1980 Kuhn House (Renovation), Beverly Hills, California
1979 Swann House, Scotts Valley, California
1974 Carey House, Grafton, Vermont
1974 Katz House, Dummerston, Vermont
1974 Taylor House, Westminster West, Vermont
1970 Rostane House, Okamiden, Morocco

Faculty Positions

1997 Faculty, Woodbury University (Nick Seierup), Burbank, California
1997 Coordinadora Latinoamericana de Estudiantes de Arquitectura (Symposium), Caracas, Venezuela
1997 Fourth International Symposium of Architecture, Universidad Automa de Nuevo Leon, Monterrey, Mexico
1985 Faculty, Graduate School of Architecture, University of California at Los Angeles, Los Angeles, California
1983 Faculty, Southern California Institute of Architecture, Santa Monica, California
1982–83 Faculty, University of Southern California, Los Angeles, California
1974–77 Faculty, Ahmadu Bello University, Zaria, Nigeria
1972 Faculty, Montana State University, Bozeman, Montana

[THIS BOOK IS DEDICATED TO MY MOM]

Acknowledgments

The Work: Without everyone past and present in our architectural family at Steven Ehrlich Architects (SEA) who have the talent and energy to produce the buildings they believe in, this work would not come to be.

Nick Seierup, my partner and principal Your talents are many, ranging from design to business. I'm proud to forge ahead together.

Gary Alzona, Jim Schmidt, and Tom Zahlten, associates You make these buildings happen from computer screen to meritorious work in the field. Thank you for your years of energy.

John Gerard, architect You're always there. Thank you.

Scott Hunter, Richard Lin, Ursula Kachler, Cecily Young New blood, energy, and talent will always keep us searching.

Ellenita Goulding, bookkeeper Thank you for keeping the numbers flowing and accurate. Please stay for five more years.

Jacqueline Filipowicz, office manager, and Onna Ehrlich, assistant It's not easy being the nerve center at SEA. Thank you for always maintaining composure.

Interns from all over the world You bring to us limitless energy and enthusiasm

The Book: Certain key people provided the inspiration and support to make this book a reality.

David Morton, senior editor at Rizzoli Thank you for your belief in our work. You made this book possible and I am grateful.

Tracey Shiffman, book's designer You taught me how to see architecture in a new way and how it must jump out onto the page with strength and vision. You're tough and I love you.

Joseph Giovannini, architecture critic and writer I learned a great deal from your insights, observations, and comparisons. Your steadfast belief in integrity and clarity will help guide us.

Jack Prichett, consulting editor and writer of texts You always are able to write in a way that makes a complex concept tangible and understandable to everyone. Thank you for your years of friendship.

Ron Broadhurst, editorial assistant at Rizzoli You truly put this entire monograph together. Thank you for your insight and patience.

Photographers (see p. 232) Thank you for your magic.

The Clients: I want to thank my clients past, present, and future. It's impossible to include everyone, so I thank these and many others not mentioned here. These people are the producers of these projects. Without their belief in us we could not do our life's work.

ACADEMIC
Orange Coast College: Ted Baker, Jim McIlwain, Margaret Gratton, Gene Farrell, Doug Bennett, Rick Steadry, Wayne Tennant

Crossroads School: Paul Cummins, David Paul

California State University Fullerton: Mike McGee, Jay Bond

CIVIC
Redevelopment Agency of the City of San Jose: Frank Taylor, Tom Aidala, Jeff Oberdorfer, Mark Patrosso

City of Los Angeles: Bill Holland, May Woo, Connie Gacad, Fontaine Holmes, Leslie Nordby

ENTERTAINMENT
DreamWorks SKG: Jeffrey Katzenberg, Terry Press, Sandy Rabins, Dave Mannix, Mike Montgomery, Rob Vogel, Todd Conversano, Rinaldo Vezilzia

Sony Pictures: Ken Williams, Barbara Cline, Bob Sirchia

Sony Music: Tommy Mattola, Don Burkhimer, Bob Lowe, Rick Newman, Rob MacLeod

Warner Bros.: Dan Garcia, John Matthews

Universal: David Glover

Ten9Fifty/Skye Partners: Greg Harless, Brad Dingwell

ARTIST'S STUDIOS
Guy Dill
Renee & Jordan Kalfus
Ed Moses
John Okulick

COMMERCIAL
Broadway Deli: Bruce Marder, Marvin Ziedler, Michel Richard

BUS: Brian Cinadr, Richard and Agnes Thayler

World Savings: Marion and Herbert Sandler, Jay Watt, Stephen Shapiro, Jerry Kirkpatrick

Futiko-Tamagowon: Mr. Arai, Tomo Hayashida

HOUSES (WITH LOVE)
Bill and Laurie Benenson
Bob Doroux
Lisa Richards and Michael Ebert
Rick Ehrman and Philip Coombs
Perry Farrell
Ellen and Harvey Friedman
John Friedman and Jeanie Gold
Hannah Hempstead
David and Lindy Israel
Enid and Stephen Koffler
John Law and Hope Warschaw
Arthur and May Lo
Sylvia and Robert Lowe
Lionel and Andy Margolin
Paul Miller and Peggy Nazarey
Ann and Barry Munitz
Robert and Laurie Plattner
Ian and Barbara Robertson
Tom and Miriam Schulman
Steven and Kathleen St. John
Howard Swann
Jan and Eddie Woods

The Collaborators: I thank the executive architects, landscape architects, artists, engineers, contractors, and the men and women who built these projects.

The Life: My kids—Julia, Vanessa, Onna, and Laura—nourish me and help keep my life's work in a happy perspective.

My wife, Marlo, my mother, Betty, my sister, Renée, my family, and special friends make it possible for me to follow my dreams.

Chris Allaire
Jah Ansavananda
Gantcho Batchkarov
Mel Bernstein
Mitch Bjorum
Gloria Bonner
Steven Bradbury
Darko Brezak
Edward Carfagno
Nadine Carome
Timothy Champ
Un-Ju Choi
Todd Conversano
Gina Deeming
Brent Eckerman
Emmeline Elzin
Zazu Faure
Todd Flournoy
Philip Gamble
Andreas Gritschke
Eric Hammerlund
Stephanie Hinsen
Markus Hintzen
Tina Hollenbacher
Don Holtz
Milica Jaksic
Steve Karolyi
Richard Katkov
Supachai Kiatkwankul
Carlos Kitzinger
Anja Koch
Frederic LeClercq

Sookja Lee
Mei-Ting Lin
Kathleen McMahon
Matthew Miller
Bruce Morrison
Yuki Murata
Hans Osterman
Carlos Lahoz Palacio
Pierre Paley
Stephanie Pennix
Jan Portugal
Erin Possel
Susanne Proesl
Glen Rappaport
Iris Anna Regn
Jonathan Riddle
Andy Rovelstad
Leon Saperstein
Kim Sapida
Martin Schwartz
Mohammed Sharif
Eric Stultz
Christina Sverzuti
Karen Thornton
Jeff Turner
Rinaldo Veseliza
Andy Waisler
Lisa Weeks
Rasa Wheeler
Troy Williams
Marlo Wolfe
Jenny Wu
Juergen Zimmerman

CURRENT TEAM

Steven Ehrlich, FAIA, *principal*
Nick Seierup, AIA, *principal*

James Schmidt, AIA, *associate*
Thomas Zahlten, AIA, *associate*
Gary Alzona, *associate*

Rita Chang
Onna Ehrlich
Jacqueline Filipowicz
John Gerard
Ellenita Goulding
Scott Hunter, AIA
Ursula Kachler
Richard Lin
Natalie Tan
Charles Whitten III
Cecily Young, AIA

Illustration Credits

Tom Bonner: 4, 6 (middle), 8 (fig. 6), 10 (fig. 9), 11 (fig. 11), 13 (fig. 16), 14 (fig. 19), 17, 18, 19, 20–21, 23, 24, 25, 27, 28, 29, 30–31, 32, 34, 35, 36, 37, 54, 55, 56, 57, 58, 59, 60–61, 83, 90–91, 93, 94, 97, 98–99, 100, 101, 103, 154, 156, 160–61, 162, 163 (bottom), 166, 167, 168, 169, 170, 171, 172–73, 175, 176, 177, 178, 179 (top), 180–81, 182, 183, 215 (fig. 8), 217 (figs. 12, 13), 232

Gregory Cloud: 10 (fig. 10), 12 (fig. 14), 76, 77, 87 (top), 147, 206, 208, 210, 213

Grey Crawford: 81, 110, 118, 119, 121, 122, 124, 126, 128, 133, 134, 136, 196, 199

Christopher Dow: 138, 141, 142, 143, 144, 179 (bottom), 198

Steven Ehrlich: 6 (top), 7 (figs. 1–4), 8 (fig. 5), 11 (fig. 12), 68, 70, 71, 74–75 (except insets), 111, 163 (top), 204 (bottom), 205 (bottom), 214, 215 (figs. 4, 6, 7), 216 (figs. 9, 11), 217 (fig. 16), 218 (figs. 17–20), 219 (figs. 21–24), 220 (figs. 25–27), 221 (figs. 28, 29)

Sonja Foncesca: 129

Dennis Freppel: 51

K. Furdate: 62, 63, 65, 66, 67

Michael Garland: 194–95

John Edward Linden: 82, 88 (top)

Lawrence Manning: 69, 73, 74–75 (insets), 139, 190, 192, 193, 216 (fig. 10), 221 (fig. 30)

Michael C. McMillen: 222–23, 231

Ministry du l'urbanisme et l'habitat Morocco: 215 (fig. 5), 217 (fig. 14, 15)

Grant Mudford: 9

Erhard Pfeifer: 12 (fig. 15), 44, 45, 46, 47, 50, 52

Tim Street Porter: 6 (bottom), 8 (fig. 7), 87 (bottom), 112, 114, 115, 116, 117, 153, 184, 186, 187

Claudio Santini: 127

Julius Shulman: 185, 188–89

Julius Shulman and David Glomb: 84, 85, 88 (bottom), 89

Adrian Villascecu: 13 (fig. 17), 14 (fig. 18), 38, 40–41, 42, 200, 202–203, 204 (top), 205 (top)

Alan Weintraub: 92, 96, 104, 106, 107, 108, 109, 130, 132, 135, 137